Earned Value

Project Management

Second Edition

Earned Value

Project Management

Second Edition

Quentin W. Fleming
Joel M. Koppelman

Project Management Institute
Newtown Square, Pennsylvania USA

Library of Congress Cataloging-in-Publication Data

Fleming, Quentin W.
    Earned value project management / Quentin W. Fleming and Joel M. Koppelman.--2nd ed.
        p.   cm.
    Includes index.
    ISBN: 1-880410-27-3 (alk. paper)
    1. Cost control. 2. Program budgeting. 3. Production control. 4. Industrial project
management. I. Koppelman, Joel M. II. Title.

    HD47.3 .F59 2000
    658.15--dc21   00-055864
                                                          CIP

ISBN: 1-880410-27-3

Published by: Project Management Institute, Inc.
                Four Campus Boulevard
                Newtown Square, Pennsylvania 19073-3299 USA.
                Phone: 610-356-4600 or Visit our website: www.pmi.org

PMI® books are available at quantity discounts. For more information, please write to the
Publisher, PMI Publishing, Four Campus Boulevard, Newtown Square, PA 19073-3299 USA.
Call: (610) 356-4600 or visit your local bookstore.

The paper used in this book complies with the Permanent Paper Standard issued by the National
Information Standards Organization (Z39.48-1984).

10 9 8 7 6 5 4 3

Contents

List of Figures

Introduction

The first release of this book was in October 1996 at the Project Management Institute's 27th Annual Seminars & Symposium in Boston. We had a single objective for our effort: to describe the earned value concept in a simple manner so that it could be applied to any project, of any size, and in any industry. Earned value project management ... for the masses!

It was also our goal to build on the fine work of the United States Department of Defense (DOD) with earned value as a central part of what it called the Cost/Schedule Control Systems Criteria (C/SCSC). The DOD had accumulated data on earned value applications that had transformed the concept into a significant management science.

However, within two months after the release of this book, in December 1996, the DOD canceled its C/SCSC and accepted the industry rewrite of the criteria. Gone were the "dumb" terms of "Budgeted Costs for Work Scheduled" (BCWS) and "Budgeted Costs for Work Performed" (BCWP) that most project managers and executives flatly rejected using over the years. In their place were terms people could comprehend, like "earned value."

The rewrite of the criteria by industry was not a revolutionary change but rather an evolutionary process improvement. The National Security Industrial Association's (NSIA) subcommittee on management systems provided leadership for this work. The intent of the NSIA subcommittee was to transfer the ownership of earned value from the government to private industry. It was successful. It termed its rewrite: Earned Value Management Systems (EVMS). It was an important improvement in the formal earned value process.

An unofficial authors' description of the revised EVMS criteria and a comparison between the thirty-five old and thirty-two new criteria are included as appendices to this update. Later, in 1998, these same industry EVMS criteria were accepted as an American National Standards Institute/ Electronic Industry Association standard, called ANSI/EIA 748.

However, as it was with the earlier C/SCSC, it remains the opinion of the authors that the employment of all EVMS criteria is more than most projects need in order to utilize the earned value concept. We have attempted to identify the minimum requirements that we feel are necessary to use earned value as a simple tool for project managers.

We have also witnessed the use of simple earned value on software projects and find that particularly exciting. Realistically, a Cost Performance Index (CPI) is the same whether the project is a multibillion-dollar high-technology project, or a simple one hundred thousand-dollar software project. A CPI is a CPI ... period. It is a solid metric that reflects the heath of the project.

This is not a new book, but rather it is an updated book. However, we have made some important additions. In many cases, there will be no changes to a given section. But in other sections, we have made substantial revisions to what we had described earlier. Our goal remains the same with this update: describe earned value project management in its most fundamental form, for application to all projects, of any size or complexity.

Quentin W. Fleming　　　　　　　　Joel M. Koppelman
Tustin, California 92780　　　　　　Bala Cynwyd, Pennsylvania 19004

Chapter 1

Earned Value Project Management ... An Introduction*

"Earned value" is a project management technique that is emerging as a valuable tool in the management of all projects, including and in particular software projects. In its most simple form earned value equates to fundamental project management. Here these authors describe the technique in a storybook form. It is not necessarily a true story ... but it could be.

Once upon a time there was a young man who wanted to be a project manager. Don't ask us why.

In school, the young man took the most challenging of the technical subjects, but he also liked to manage things. He graduated with a master's degree in a technical discipline and immediately went to work for a small but fast-growing hi-tech company. This company was a leader in developing new products for its niche of the market. It had just gone public, and its initial public offering of the stock was a huge financial success. The young man knew that he had joined the right company. All he wanted was his chance at bat. He wanted to be a project manager.

A year went by ... a whole year. And he had yet to receive an assignment of any consequence. He was becoming discouraged. He considered up-

*This chapter is a reprint of an article that appeared in the July 1999 issue of *Crosstalk, the Journal of Defense Software Engineering,* published by the Software Technology Support Center, Hill Air Force Base, Ogden, Utah.

dating his résumé to start looking around. If his present employer did not recognize his talents, perhaps others would. He did not have time to waste. He was in a hurry.

Then one day, as he was walking down the hall, the chief executive (CEO) came up to him. She inquired how he was getting along. Then she asked: "How would you like an important assignment as manager of a development project?" The young man could hardly get out his enthusiastic acceptance. Then the CEO said: "OK, if you're interested, call my secretary and get on my calendar for first thing in the morning." As she was walking away, she commented to him: "This is an extremely important project for the company, and I think you could manage it nicely. See you then."

Our young man got little sleep that night. Imagine ... his chance to actually manage a project, to be a project manager. He was in the CEO's office a full thirty minutes before she arrived. When they met, she started by saying: "This is one of the most important potential new products we have in the pipeline, but it needs some innovative thinking, and that's why I think you would be the right person to take this on. I need fresh ideas incorporated into this product."

She outlined the concept for the new product, and it was exactly the type of work that he had prepared himself to do. She asked him to gather a half dozen cross-functional people from within the company and prepare a project plan for her approval. "If you have any problem getting people, use my name to break them loose. I don't want stonewalling by anyone; this product is important to our future growth."

Then she closed the meeting by saying: "The time to market is most critical on this project. I know others are working on it, and I want to be first into the marketplace." The young man got the message, and it was better than he had ever hoped. On his way out, she mentioned another issue: "I would also like you to use a technique I have heard about but can't seem to get it started here ... earned value management. Have you ever heard of it?"

"Yes, of course; we studied it in school, and I think it would work well on this project," was his reply.

"Good; I look forward to seeing your performance plan," was her closing remark.

The young man circulated within the company and got the commitment of the right people to do the planning job. This was a young start-up company so that the "brick walls" so pervasive in older more-established companies had not yet set in. All he had to do was mention that the big boss was behind this assignment, and he got his people. He didn't even have to describe the details of the assignment; they all knew it had a high priority.

Planning for Earned Value Project Management

The team met at his apartment to prevent interruptions and phone calls. "It shouldn't take us very long to put a plan on paper," was his opening remark. The team members spent the day conceptualizing and defining the project. After he solicited their ideas, the project manager would prepare the final plan for review and approval of the team prior to sub-mittal to the CEO. The project manager wanted everyone to buy-in to the project plan. They all knew exactly what was required in order to employ earned value performance measurement. It was simply classic project man-agement, "Project Management 101."

First, team members had to define what constituted 100 percent of their assumed project scope. For this, they used a "Work Breakdown Structure" (WBS) diagram. Next they would decompose the project scope into measurable tasks, each with an estimated value, and then assign re-sponsibility for actual performance to some functional manager within the company. For this, and to record their thoughts, they used a "WBS dic-tionary." They knew that their project had ten units to develop and test, and that each unit would require about the same level of resources to ac-complish.

Next they would take the work broadly conceptualized from the WBS diagram and dictionary, and then do a detailed plan and schedule for all the major critical tasks. After a few iterations, they had their "Project Master Schedule" (PMS) fully supported by critical path methodology. They did a forward and backward schedule pass to provide assurances that their PMS was in fact viable. The project would take eighteen months to perform from go-ahead to completion.

Lastly, they estimated the resources required to produce these ten units, which constituted the total project. Each article would cost $150,000 to produce; thus, the total project would run $1.5 million dollars to complete. They charted their requirements, as illustrated in Figure 1.1, which they termed their "Project Management Plan." This display would contain the three critical elements of the plan: WBS, PMS, and a "Performance Display" graph. Each element was supported by de-tailed breakouts. This process is typically called "bottoms-up planning." The team members had done their job, and it was now time for the project manager to take their plan to the CEO for her approval.

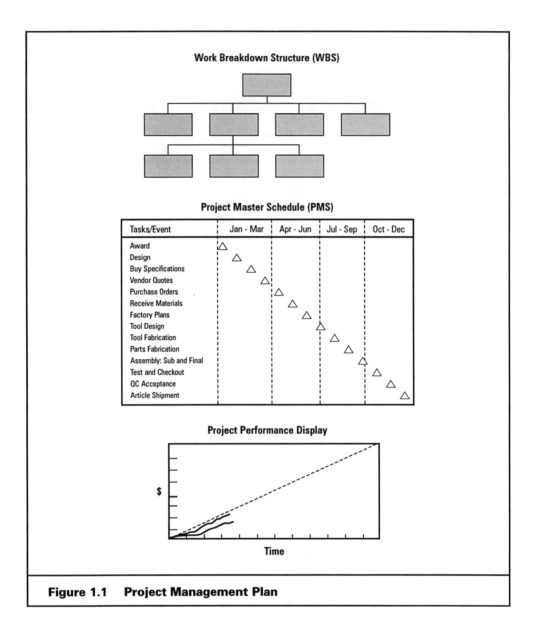

Figure 1.1   Project Management Plan

Management's Approval

The project manager made a copy of the team's project management plan and gave it to the CEO's secretary so that the CEO could review it prior to the approval meeting. When he was, at last, able to meet with the CEO, it was obvious that she had thoroughly read the entire plan ... everything was marked and color-coded. He hoped that she liked what she had read.

The CEO opened on a positive note: "This is the finest internal project management plan I have ever seen as head of this company, and we will use it as a model for all our future projects to follow." The project manager was off to a good start. She liked it!

Then the CEO went on: "However, you must not have heard parts of my requirements. Time to market is most critical on this project, and you are projecting a casual schedule of eighteen months; that is completely unacceptable. I need this project completed in not more that twelve months. Can you handle that?"

The young man took a deep breath and said: "Of course, we can." He had no clue how he would do this, but the message from high was becoming pretty clear.

"Also, I think you have gold plated this job at a cost of $1.5 million; that also is unacceptable!" The boss was relentless: "The very most I could allocate for this project would be $1 million. We are not a big company; I have other commitments. Can you handle that?"

The young project manager was beginning to understand why she had become CEO at such an early age ... she was one tough person to deal with. Without hesitation, the young man accepted the budget dictate.

The CEO realized that she had come down pretty hard on the young man, so she wanted to provide some consoling words before he left: "Again I want to emphasize that this is the best project plan that I have ever seen in this company; it will be our role model for others to follow."

Her words were some comfort, although the project manager was now starting to worry about what he would say to the other members of his team. Their buy-in was essential to him.

As he was leaving the office, the CEO said: "I am very pleased that you are going to employ earned value measurement on this project. I would like to review your performance each quarter, at, say, three months into your twelve-month project!"

She never lets up, was the thought racing through his mind. What do I now tell the others?

Welcome to the World of Project Management

Now let us stand back from this situation and try to assess what took place here. Project team members got together and developed a thorough, comprehensive project plan with sufficient supporting data and schedule metrics, so that the members could measure their earned value performance from start to completion. In particular, they had scoped 100 percent of the total assumed project before they would begin to perform and created a plan that could be measured. Good.

Their supporting bottoms-up detail indicated that they needed eighteen months to complete the project, and the big boss directed them to do it in twelve months. They estimated the costs to do the project at $1.5 million, and the big boss cut it to $1 million. What do we call this environment that the young project manager has just experienced for the first time in his life? We call it: REAL-LIFE PROJECT MANAGEMENT!

Rarely do we ever get the total time that we feel we need to reasonably do the job. Projects are always in competition with others to do something first. And the authorized budgets are rarely what we estimate we need to complete any job. We are frequently given what is termed a "management challenge," and we go out and do our best. It matters not if these management challenges are arbitrary, unreasonable, unattainable, unrealistic, stupid, and so forth. We as project managers must find a way to get them done. Welcome to the world of project management.

The First Quarterly Project Status Review

Three months went by, and it was now time for the team to present its performance results to the CEO and the management committee. This would be an awesome new experience for the young project team, but the thing that was working in its favor was the fact that it was performing to a detailed plan, and the members knew exactly what they had to do from the go-ahead.

A brief summary of their results indicated the following: Three units had been scheduled for completion at the three-month point, but only two were accomplished; thus, they were slightly behind with their planned schedule. They had forecasted expenditures of $300,000 and had committed $300,000, so that they were right on their funding profile. An optimistic person could easily paint a positive picture of this project: "We are a little behind schedule, we are right on our spend plan; leave us alone, and life will be good," would be the spin put on these results by most practitioners.

However, the CEO had specifically asked that earned value project management be employed on this project, and that requires a slightly different orientation toward these same project performance data. Earned value management requires a detailed bottoms-up performance plan, measurement taken against one's own plan, and a periodic forecast of the final expected results, based on actual performance results. Earned value requires detailed measurement against the project plan.

In order to employ earned value, we must have a plan in place that will allow us to continuously measure seven points of data. This may sound complicated and cumbersome, but it is not. It is simply the kind of data most projects have, but we may not look at the data in quite the same way. Earned value has a focus on its percent-complete position ... against its (100 percent) defined scope.

In order to employ earned value we must first know at all times what the "planned value" is as at any point in time. (**Note**: The United States Department of Defense [DOD] has been calling this the "Budgeted Costs for Work Scheduled" [BCWS] for some three decades, but we choose to call it simply the planned value.) To determine this, we need to focus on two issues.

To establish the planned value, we must determine 1) how much physical or intellectual work we have scheduled to be completed as of the point of measurement. This is a direct fallout of those detailed tasks contained from our PMS. (**Important Point**: Earned value requires a master project schedule, or, stated another way, without a master project schedule one cannot perform earned value management.) In this case, the PMS described three units to be accomplished as of the measurement period.

Second, we need to determine 2) what was the budgeted value of the work scheduled. We were authorized $100,000 per unit, so that our budgeted value for work scheduled was $300,000. Thus, we have set our planned value for the first three months of the project at $300,000.

(**Note**: The fact that we had originally estimated that each unit would require $150,000 to accomplish is only interesting. Management has actually authorized $100,000 per unit and thus doesn't want to hear about other issues ... period! Best to forget the $150,000 issue!)

Next we will want to measure our earned value for the reporting period. To measure earned value we need two new points of data, which we will call items 3 and 4.

As of the reporting period, 3) how much of our scheduled work have we actually accomplished? We examine our PMS and find that we have accomplished two of the three units that we originally scheduled. The third unit has not been worked.

Next, 4) what is the budgeted value of the work actually performed? In this case, we were authorized $100,000 per unit, so that our earned value for the reporting period is $200,000. (Never mind actual costs at this point ... they will only confuse the issue.) Thus, items 3 and 4 constitute our earned value for the reporting period. (**Note**: The DOD has typically has called this the BCWP.)

The next item that we need to determine is, for the earned value work we have accomplished, what 5) costs have we actually spent and/or incurred. We look at our cost ledger and find that we have incurred actual costs of $300,000.

We now have our earned value results for the first quarter, quantified in dollar terms, and a performance pattern is starting to emerge:

> The Planned Value = $300,000, items 1 and 2
> The Earned Value = $200,000, items 3 and 4
> Actual Costs = $300,000, item 5

We now need to ascertain our project performance variances, which is a slightly different look at data with earned value measurement.

Next issue: We need to understand 6) the "schedule variance," which in earned value is the difference between our planned value scheduled and our earned value achieved. In this case, we planned to accomplish $300,000 worth of work, but only did $200,000, so that we are behind our planned schedule by $100,000. Not so bad until we realize that we only accomplished sixty-seven cents for each dollar that we planned to do!

Lastly, we need to know 7) what our "cost variances" have been. This is determined by relating our earned value accomplished against the actual costs spent or incurred. Thus, we spent $300,000 in actual costs to accomplish $200,000 in earned value! Not so good when we realize that for each dollar we spent, we got only sixty-seven cents of value earned.

The team summarizes the results of its earned value performance for presentation to the management committee. Not exactly a pretty sight, but one of extreme importance in the portrayal of the true status of project performance. This project at the end of the first quarter is earning only 67 percent of its planned schedule and is overrunning its costs by 50 percent. At the 20 percent completion point, by monitoring earned value data, it is forecasting a significant final overrun!

If the project continues its present "cost efficiency" rate of earning only sixty-seven cents for each dollar spent, it would need plus 50 percent more budget to complete the work ($1,000,000/.67 = $1,5000,000). If it also tries to get back on the twelve-month schedule, as directed by management, it will have to add additional resources to do the same work, so that the projected costs would equate to a 100 percent overrun.

Most senior executives do not like to hear bad news. But this CEO knew that bad news does not improve with time; it only gets worse. At issue: Bad news known at the 20 percent point in a project's life cycle gives management an opportunity to take corrective actions and possibly alter the final results. Conversely, bad news that is ignored, or not addressed until perhaps the 80 percent completion point, severely limits management's opportunities to make the necessary changes to recover performance. Earned value provides an "early warning" signal.

This was exactly the kind of performance results that the CEO wanted to see on this most critical project. She wanted the truth, good or bad. She now declared: "Thank you for this presentation, it has been most informative. I now know that I was perhaps a little too arbitrary in my initial budget authorization to you. I will authorize a revised budget amount of $1,500,000 to complete this project."

"Thank you" was the surprised response from the young project manager. He knew that the team needed at least that amount to complete this project.

(Authors' comment: One of the primary reasons why earned value results become so reliable at the early phases of a project's life cycle—at the 15 to 20 percent point in the project's life cycle—rests on the human nature side of the planning process. If you have a period of performance extending one cycle, where will you likely place your best planning ... in the early periods or in the later periods? Answer: Likely, in the early periods, and hope for the best in the later periods. Also, if one has a severe budget challenge, where will the most adequate budget be distributed ... in the early or late periods of the project? Answer: Likely in the early periods. It is human nature to provide the best planning and the best resources to the early periods, and hope for the best [perhaps changes?]. Thus, the results of earned value performance measurement have been found to be most reliable, even at the early periods, say 15 percent, of the life cycle of a project.)

"However"—the CEO was not going to let anyone off the hook just yet—"I want you to catch up on the late schedule position, and bring us a completed project in another nine months. Can you do that?"

"Yes, we can, but it will take an accelerated schedule, and that will likely cost us the full $2,000,000 as we have presented to you," was the project manager's reply.

"OK, I will authorize this project a total budget of $1,500,000, but ask that you complete it within the twelve-month schedule," were the directions of the CEO. "However, as we both well know, recovering this behind-schedule condition will likely cost us some money, so I will put another half a million dollars in my management reserve in case we need it. But it is not your money yet, and we want you back on schedule. Am I making myself clear?" asked the CEO.

"Absolutely clear, and we promise to do the best we can for the authorized budget," said the project manager.

"But getting back on schedule is your main performance objective, and the budget goal is simply my management challenge to you. Understand, the schedule comes first," was the final comment from the CEO.

"Understood" said the young project manager, who was starting to appreciate the delicate role that he was playing.

The Value of Earned Value

Standing back from this situation, what was happening was that this project was likely underbudgeted (at $1,000,000) from the start. But based on what was authorized and what the project performance was experiencing, the likely final forecast of budget needs was in the statistical range of between a half million to one full million over the official budget. Both the project manager and the CEO clearly understood that fact. But the CEO was not ready to relax her management challenge to this team. She released an additional half a million dollars to the project, but asked that the team also get back on schedule. Getting back on schedule would cost additional resources and likely require the full million to achieve. But she was not yet ready to authorize the full amount.

This CEO knew the benefits of employing earned value. She believed the accuracy of data that was being reviewed by the project team and the final projections of required costs. At the 20 percent completion point, the team was predicting an overrun of between 50 to 100 percent, and she was convinced that this would ultimately be the case. In order to fund the completion of this critical company project, she took immediate steps to cancel two other internal projects of lesser importance to the company. She knew what she had to do in order to fund this highest-priority project. Other executives who do not employ earned value, or who do not rely on the performance data, often find themselves overly committed in their project portfolios, sometimes experiencing catastrophic results.

This project was completed with all of the features, on time, within the twelve-month mandated schedule, but at a final cost of close to $2,000,000 at completion. The new product worked exactly as required, and the additional funds to complete the project were made available by the CEO canceling two other projects of lesser importance.

Life was good at this company, and the young project manager's professional career was off to a good start.

Chapter 2

Earned Value Project Management ... An Overview

This book is about the management of projects. However, it will discuss the management of projects while employing an approach often referred to as the earned value concept. Hence, we will deliberately use the term "earned value project management" throughout this book to describe what we have in mind.

The concept of earned value has been around for over a hundred years, or perhaps for only three decades, depending on how one counts the beginning. Over the years, it has gone by various titles including industrial factory standards, earned value management, performance measurement, the Planned Value of Work Accomplished (PVWA), the Budgeted Costs of Work Performed (BCWP), the Cost/Schedule Control Systems Criteria (C/SCSC), the Cost/Schedule Planning Control Specification (C/SPCS), the criteria, Program Evaluation and Review Technique (PERT)/costs, and other unmentionable titles.

Whatever term has been used, the focus of earned value has been consistent: the accurate measurement of physical performance against a detailed plan to allow for the accurate prediction of the final costs and schedule results for a given project. Earned value is based on an integrated management approach that provides an indicator of true cost performance available in no other project management technique. Earned value requires that the project's scope be fully defined, and then a bottoms-up baseline plan be put in place that integrates the scope with the authorized resources, all set within a specific time frame for performance.

In terms of the proponents or opponents of the concept, there appears to be little middle ground. Some individuals feel that the technique provides a valuable tool holding considerable potential, which should be employed in the management of all projects. Others are adamantly opposed to earned value, perhaps based on some prior personal bad experience with it. This group will suggest that the effort required to employ earned value far exceeds any utility gained from using the technique. To these individuals, we respectfully suggest that they try earned value in a simplified form. They may just find a valuable new tool to better manage their projects.

We find ourselves generally in the first camp. We do like the concept, but we also have some definite reservations based on its past employment. It is our feeling that the earned value concept holds considerable promise for broad-based project management applications, but only in a simple, more user-friendly model than has been mandated in the past. Our reasoning: the requirements to oversee the performance of major new systems being acquired for government agencies on cost-reimbursable-type contracts are vastly different from the more typical needs of most project managers today. The latter group will normally commit to its projects on a fixed-price basis, within a finite authorization of company resources. Project management tools must be conceptually simple and easy to use, or they will be ignored.

A rhetorical question: If the earned value concept is an effective technique ... why has it not been embraced universally by the project managers of the world? It is our firm belief that earned value has been avoided, sometimes flatly rejected, by project managers because the technique has been "encased" for the past three decades in countless nonvalue-added regulations and esoteric interpretations of implementation requirements. This has not been project management, but rather bureaucratic dictates carried to extremes.

For almost thirty years earned value has been a part of what has been called Cost/Schedule Control Systems Criteria. What started originally as a simple concept used on the factory floor evolved into a sort of exclusive association in which one had to be specifically trained in the use of a cumbersome new vocabulary in order to be a member of this select group. Most project managers are interested only in completing their projects according to the approved plan, and have neither the time nor the inclination to master a new vernacular. Often they rightfully rejected the concept in total rather than adopt it in its more rigid form. What a shame, for by rejecting this conceptually simple but most effective cost-management technique, project managers have missed an opportunity to employ a powerful tool that can complement their other management tools, in particular, critical path method (CPM) scheduling.

Please note that it is not the purpose of this book to demean in any way what was originally the C/SCSC. As used by the United States (U.S.) government and other governments in the procurement of their "major system" acquisitions—where all of the risk of all cost growth was on them because they chose to employ a cost-reimbursable or incentive-type contract—C/SCSC was the perfect vehicle. C/SCSC has been successful as a government-required mandate for three decades.

However, major systems acquisitions by governments likely constitute something less than 1 percent of the projects in the world. Their overall dollars may be significant, but the total numbers of such projects are nevertheless quite small. But how about the other 99 percent of the world's projects? With these projects, all risks of cost growth are not on the owners or buyers, but rather on the performers, the project managers, because they have undertaken a fixed-price commitment. All of the risks of cost growth rested squarely with them. Could these project managers not have benefited from a cost-management technique that helps them to achieve what they have committed to perform? We believe that there is considerable potential in the universal employment of a simplified, user-friendly earned value approach in the management of all projects.

It is now time to take this simple factory-management technique called earned value and employ it as it was originally intended by the industrial engineers over a century ago: to compare the "planned standards" within the work plan against the "earned standards" of the physical work actually accomplished, and then to relate the "earned standards" against the "actual costs" incurred to perform the work, in order to precisely measure the true performance of our projects.

The Earned Value Concept in a Nutshell

There is nothing inherently difficult about the earned value concept. It does not require extensive training to grasp the fundamentals. In fact, many people are using some form of earned value in their daily routines and are not even aware that they are employing the concept.

For example, most construction-type projects will have someone responsible for performing work that they call cost engineering, which in other industries may be called project controls, management controls, and so on. Anytime a construction cost engineer takes the time to verify that the physical work was actually accomplished on payment invoices being processed prior to paying a supplier, the cost engineer is utilizing a simple form of earned value. He or she is focusing on the critical relationship between the actual costs being expended against the physical work actually done on the project. Cost engineers focus on the true cost performance: what we got ... for what we *spent*.

The earned value concept requires that a project performance measurement plan be created, called the planned value, typically defined with use of the project's scheduling system, and then the earned value measured against the planned value, also with use of the project's scheduling system. The physical earned value performed is then related to the actual costs spent to accomplish the physical work, providing a measure of the project's true cost performance.

Earned value provides project managers with a type of "early-warning" buzzer that sounds, allowing them to take the necessary corrective action should the project be spending more money than it is physically accomplishing. Such warning signals become available to management as early as 15 to 20 percent into a new project, in ample time to take corrective measures to alter an unfavorable outcome.

Traditional Project Cost and Funding Management

Probably the best way to understand the earned value concept is to discuss a few specific examples. To illustrate the concept, we will contrast the earned value method against the more traditional approach toward the management of project costs. Under the traditional cost and funding management approach, a new spending plan will be formulated by the project manager for review and approval by senior management. We will use as our examples the same values contained in the introductory story of the young project manager implementing the one million-dollar internal development project described in Chapter 1.

Shown in Figure 2.1 is an assumed project cost-expenditure spending plan. It displays a $1,000,000 project over a one-year time period. The projected expenditures for the first quarter forecasted an amount of $300,000 for the first quarter. The chief executive officer (CEO) reviewed the plan and gave approval for this new internally funded project. Management expects the project manager to stay within the limits of the $1,000,000 commitment, and to continuously monitor the performance during the life of the twelve-month project.

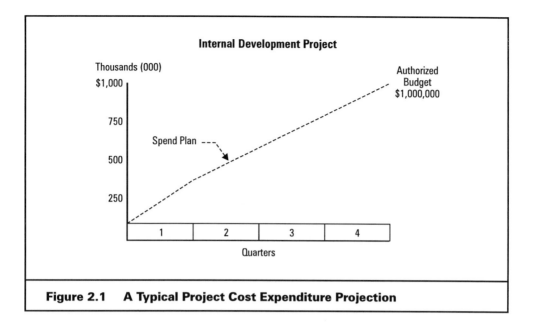

Figure 2.1   A Typical Project Cost Expenditure Projection

Using a traditional approach, at the end of the first quarter, the project manager would display the cost performance for the benefit of management, as illustrated in Figure 2.2. The approved spend plan called for an expenditure of $300,000 for the first quarter, and results thus far show an expenditure of only $300,000. One could conclude without further review that the project was performing exactly to its financial plan: $300,000 planned and $300,000 spent. Perfect cost performance. A fairly typical but unfortunately potentially deceptive approach to cost management.

In fact, nobody could really determine the project's true cost performance status by use of the display shown in Figure 2.2. To determine the true project performance, one would need to compare the schedule status alongside of the costs' status. But if the project's cost support organization developed its displays using one approach—perhaps with a breakout of costs by function—and the scheduling people developed their charts using another approach—perhaps reflecting work tasks—the two displays of cost and schedule would not match each other. It is difficult or perhaps impossible to relate the true cost and schedule status when these two key functional groups develop their respective plans using different assumptions. But it is fairly common practice to do so.

However, an interesting observation: Most of the projects in the world today would likely display their cost status for management using a chart similar to that reflected in Figure 2.2. Further, most of the schedule

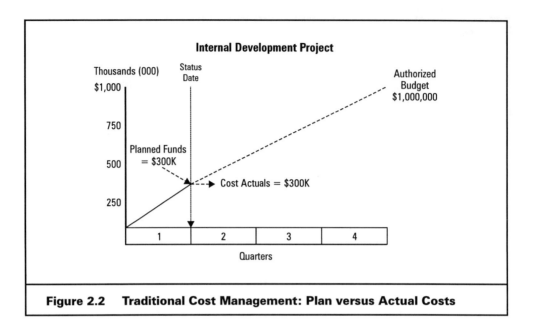

Figure 2.2   Traditional Cost Management: Plan versus Actual Costs

displays being used by projects today will not directly correlate to the cost displays provided by the finance people. Most of the projects today likely are not working to an "integrated" management approach, which allows the project to equate the defined scope to its authorized resources to the project master schedule. Earned value project management requires an integrated baseline plan that will relate the scope to costs and to the schedule.

Let us now contrast the display in Figure 2.2 with an earned value performance chart, shown in Figure 2.3. Here the total budget of $1,000,000 will be made up from detailed bottoms-up plans that allow for performance to be measured throughout the life of the project. The amount forecasted to be spent at the end of the first quarter is now labeled the "Planned Value." Performance through the first quarter called for an accomplishment of $300,000 in the value of the work scheduled.

The new third dimension of project performance that earned value provides is introduced in Figure 2.3. This display reflects actual physical earned value of only $200,000 against a planned value of $300,000. We can immediately see that the project is running behind the work that it set out to do during the first quarter. It had planned to accomplish $300,000 in work, but accomplished only $200,000. Therefore, the project can be said to be running a negative $100,000 schedule variance.

Also shown in Figure 2.3 are the cost actuals of $300,000, an amount greater than the earned value of physical work performed, $200,000. Thus, it can be inferred that this project has spent $300,000 in actual costs

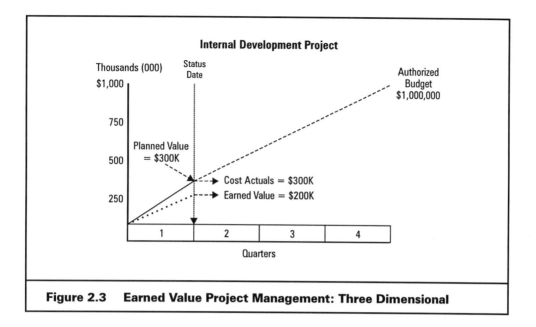

Figure 2.3   Earned Value Project Management: Three Dimensional

to achieve only $200,000 worth of earned value. We call this condition an "overrun." This project can be said to be running a negative $100,000 cost variance. The delicate relationship that it reflects can be used to predict the final costs and schedule results of the project with amazing accuracy.

This project is in trouble, but one could not have discerned that condition using a traditional cost-management approach. Only when earned value brought in a third dimension could we tell that we were experiencing problems, which needed to be addressed immediately by the project manager.

Traditional Cost Management versus Earned Value

There is an important and fundamental distinction between the data available for management using the traditional cost-control approach as compared to the three-dimensional data available when a project employs earned value. These critical differences are summarized in Figure 2.4, and focus on variances to the baseline plans.

Using the displays of planned expenditures versus actual expenditures, a project's true cost performance cannot be determined. With a plan versus cost actuals comparison, there is no way to ascertain how much of the physical work has been accomplished. Such displays merely represent the relationship of what was planned to be spent versus funds actually expended. The cost performance, displayed at the top of Figure 2.4, indicates

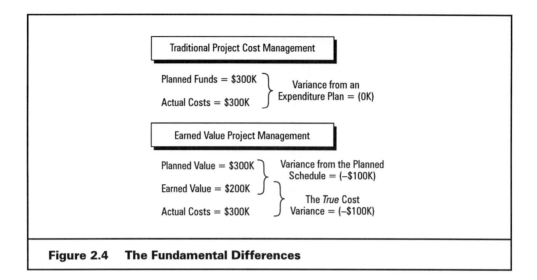

Figure 2.4   The Fundamental Differences

perfect results against the original spending plan. The utility of such displays only have significance as a reflection of whether a project has stayed within the funds authorized by management. Such charts reflect funding, not cost performance. Yet most projects typically present their cost status using a similar graphic display.

By contrast, as shown at the bottom of Figure 2.4, the earned value project displays three dimensions of data: the planned value of the work, the earned value of the physical work accomplished, and the actual costs incurred to accomplish the earned value. Thus, under an earned value approach, two critical variances may be ascertained. The first is the difference between the planned value of the work scheduled as compared to the earned value achieved. As reflected in this chart, the project is experiencing a negative schedule variance of −$100,000 from its planned work. Stated another way, one third of the work that the project set out to do was not accomplished in the time frame being measured. The project is clearly behind its planned project schedule. Such variances used in conjunction with other scheduling tools, particularly the CPM, provide valuable insight into the true schedule status of the project.

Of greater concern, however, should be the relationship of the value of the work done, the earned value, as compared to the funds expended to accomplish the work. A total of $300,000 was expended to accomplish only $200,000 worth of work. Thus, the project has experienced a cost overrun of −$100,000 for the work performed to date. This negative cost trend is of critical importance to the project, for experience has indicated that such overruns of costs do not correct themselves over time ... in fact, they tend

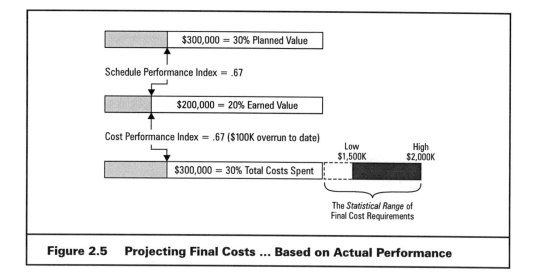

Figure 2.5   Projecting Final Costs ... Based on Actual Performance

to get worse. The actual cost and schedule results can also be used jointly to forecast the final results of the project.

Earned Value Cost and Schedule Performance Indices

Employing the earned value concept allows the project management team to monitor its own performance against a detailed time-phased plan. Exceptions to the plan provide a wealth of reliable information, primarily centered on the cost and schedule efficiency rates. Two accurate performance indices become available to the project, as early as the 15 to 20 percent point of completion. Such relationships are illustrated in Figure 2.5.

Here the three primary curves, shown in Figure 2.3, have been converted into a thermometer-type management display that reflects three dimensions of project performance as of a given point in time. Dimension one, how much project work was scheduled, answers that the planned value was $300,000 or 30 percent. Dimension two, how much work was actually performed, answers that the earned value was $200,000 or 20 percent. Dimension three, how much money was spent to achieve the earned value, answers that $300,000 or 30 percent was spent.

In this analysis, we are indebted to those who have worked with the C/SCSC concept over the past thirty years and for the body of knowledge that they have accumulated. They have scientifically demonstrated the utility of these two indices in assessing the performance of hundreds of projects, large and small, of various contract types, in various project phases, and so on.

The first issue to be determined with these results: How long will the project take to complete all of the work? The CEO authorized a one-year duration; will that happen? Using earned value metrics, we must determine what schedule-efficiency factor has been achieved for this project after the first quarter results. The project plan called for performance of $300,000 in work after the first quarter; however, only $200,000 in physical earned value was actually done. The project is the equivalent of −$100,000 behind in planned work after the first quarter. At this rate of performance, the project will likely take longer than one year to complete, unless additional resources are immediately added (more people, extensive overtime, and so on).

The amount of the earned value ($200,000) may be divided by the value of the planned work ($300,000), resulting in a planned schedule-performance efficiency factor of only .67. Stated another way, for every dollar of physical work this project had planned to accomplish, only sixty-seven cents was done. This project is said to have achieved a Schedule Performance Index (SPI) efficiency factor of .67. The SPI can be a valuable tool for use in conjunction with a CPM to forecast the expected completion date for the project. It also has utility when used in conjunction with the Cost Performance Index (CPI) to forecast the total required funds to complete the project.

Second issue to be determined: How much will the project require to complete all of the work? The CEO authorized a fixed amount of $1,000,000 to complete the project. Will this happen? To assess the required funds, we must determine the cost-efficiency factor after the first quarter. By relating the amount of physical earned value accomplished against the dollars actually spent to accomplish the earned value, one can determine the cost performance efficiency for a project. When we divide the earned value of $200,000 by the actual dollars of $300,000, we can determine that the CPI is .67 for the project. Stated another way, for every project dollar that was spent, only sixty-seven cents in physical work was accomplished. This project is said to have achieved a CPI of .67. The CPI is a powerful tool to use to predict the final costs needed to finish a job. The CPI can be used by itself or in conjunction with the SPI to forecast a statistical range of estimated final costs to complete the project.

Using the CPI and SPI to Statistically Forecast the Final Project Results

Once a project has established its CPI and SPI pattern, based on actual performance to date, what is the advantage of having or even knowing these two factors? Answer: Both the cost and schedule performance indices can be used to statistically forecast the final required funds needed to complete the project. Independent statistical forecasts can be a sort of "sanity check" on the trend and final direction of the project. They can be compared against the optimism that often prevails on projects: "Stay out of our way, and let us do our thing." Such forecasts can be developed with the CPI alone, or with the CPI used in conjunction with the SPI.

Assume that, in spite of the negative cost and schedule performance results achieved in the initial first quarter of the project, the final estimated costs by the project manager are still forecasted to be $1,000,000, the amount originally authorized by the CEO. Would this have been a reasonable forecast? Probably not, unless there were extenuating circumstances to consider. A realistic bottoms-up estimate of the remaining tasks is always the more desirable forecasting method. But bottoms-up estimates take time to prepare and distract from doing project work. A statistical forecast is but a checkpoint against such detailed forecasts.

Statistically, with earned value data, one can take the total budgeted funds of $1,000,000, divide the amount by the cumulative CPI factor of .67, and quickly statistically forecast that about $1,500,000 would be needed to complete the project. This forecasting technique has been demonstrated to represent a reliable indicator of the "minimum" total required project costs, which many feel is the very best that the project may experience.

A second method relies on the value of both the CPI (.67) times the SPI (.67), and uses the resulting product (.4489) to statistically forecast the maximum funds likely to be required to complete the job. This method incorporates the cost overrun to date with a behind-schedule condition to produce a more severe statistical forecast. The estimated amount is now something close to $2,000,000, and is considered by many to represent a "high-end" statistical method.

Thus, we can quickly create a statistical range of final cost projections between $1,500,000 to $2,000,000 needed to complete the project, and compare them with the "official" forecast provided by the project manager.

The project has already incurred an overrun of $100,000, spending $300,000 to do $200,000 worth of work. The $100,000 spent is nonrecoverable. Any differences between the project manager's forecast and these statistical estimates should be reconciled with management.

Each of these statistical formulas used to forecast final cost and schedule results will be covered in greater detail later in this book.

In Summary

While the earned value concept was officially introduced to industry some three decades ago, its applications thus far have been largely restricted to the acquisitions of major new systems by agencies of the U.S. and other governments. For some reason, the technique has not been universally embraced by the countless project managers in the private sector who also strive to perform their work in an exemplary manner.

It is the belief of the authors that the resistance to the universal adoption of the earned value concept is not the fault of the technique itself, but rather is in the implementation requirements, the terminology employed, and the countless rules and interpretations that have been rightly perceived by most project managers to be overly restrictive. We must find a way to simplify the earned value concept, reduce it to its bare essentials, if it is to be adopted as a broad-based project management tool for universal applications in all industries. We must find a balance between the utility of the technique ... versus the energy it takes to implement the concept.

That can easily be achieved by getting back to the basics that were used in the industrial factories over a century ago: by simply relating the planned standards to the earned standards to the actual costs for accomplishing the work. This book seeks to describe a simple form of earned value for the management of all projects.

Chapter 3

The Genesis and Evolution of Earned Value

Origin of Earned Value

Likely, most of us became acquainted with Earned Value Management (EVM) as it was ingrained in what was then called the Cost/Schedule Control Systems Criteria, or simply the C/SCSC. The C/SCSC constituted nothing more than thirty-five standards of compliance (criteria) that were applied against the management control systems within private industry to assure the consistency and reporting of performance on new United States (U.S.) government acquisition projects. The criteria were imposed by governmental agencies whenever they underwrote the risks of cost growth—that is, whenever they employed either a cost-reimbursable or incentive-type contract for a new development project.

The criteria were first released by the U.S. Department of Defense (DOD) in December 1967, and were consistently used as its approved method of cost management in the procurement of major new systems. Since that time, other U.S. governmental agencies and certain foreign governments adopted identical or slightly modified performance measurement criteria for application with private industry.

While the C/SCSC did encompass EVM, the C/SCSC had broader applications than simply employing earned value. We owe it to ourselves to understand the fundamental differences. The opportunities for broad-based EVM exist ... but only if the fundamentals can be extracted from within C/SCSC. Earned value as a part of the C/SCSC was too complicated, too rigid, for universal project management applications.

The earned value concept was conceived by the industrial engineers working in the early American factories, by such scientific management practitioners as Frederick W. Taylor, Frank and Lillian Gilbreth, Henry Lawrence Gantt, and others. One former U.S. Air Force general who was involved in the modern implementation of earned value over thirty years ago commented:

> The earned value concept came to us right off the factory floor, from the industrial engineers who were comparing their **planned standards** with the **earned standards** and **actual costs.** We simply applied this same concept to our one-time only, non-recurring developmental tasks (Driessnack 1993).

The favorable experience with earned value as employed initially on the Minuteman Missile program eventually led to the issuance of C/SCSC as a formal doctrine in 1967.

These thirty-five formal management-control system standards have led to the development of some rather sophisticated approaches for the monitoring of project performance. They have also provided a means to accurately predict the project's final cost requirements and time requirements, based on a project's own performance record at a given point in time. As early as 15 percent through a new project, the performance results (earned) can be used to predict the final required costs within a determinable range of values. Early into a new project, the actual cost performance efficiency factor (the earned value) has been demonstrated to be stable, providing data that can be used to predict the final costs for a given project.

If they were still with us today, the original scientific managers—Taylor, the Gilbreths, and Gantt—would be pleased with the body of scientific knowledge that has been carefully accumulated over the past three decades. In fact, certain professional management societies have incorporated some of these same findings into their professional repositories of information. Of particular significance to most of us working in the profession would likely be the Project Management Institute's document entitled *A Guide to the Project Management Body of Knowledge (PMBOK® Guide).* This universally read document describes earned value in three of its key chapters: Project Integration Management, Project Cost Management, and Project Communications Management.

Evolution of the Earned Value Concept

The earned value concept was conceived a hundred years ago sometime in the latter part of the twentieth century. For purposes of this discussion, we have somewhat arbitrarily divided the evolution of earned value into distinct phases, so that we may address each stage separately. As with any such forced classification, there are overlaps in these divisions.

Phase 0—The Factory Floor: In the Late 1800s

The earned value concept originally came from the industrial engineers working in the early American factories. For years, industrial engineers have done what most corporate executives fail to do even today: they employ a "three-dimensional" approach to assess the cost performance efficiency for work done in the factory. For years, the industrial engineers have been relating their "earned standards" actually achieved against the "actual expenses" incurred to measure the performance in their factories.

The result of this approach is EVM in its most basic form. Most important, the industrial engineers have been defining a cost variance as representing the difference between the actual costs spent ... as compared to the earned standards achieved (Moski 1951). This basic definition of a "cost variance" is perhaps the litmus test for determining whether or not one is utilizing the earned value concept.

Phase 1—PERT/Cost: 1962–65

Program Evaluation Review Technique (PERT) was first introduced to industry as a network-scheduling device by the U.S. Navy in 1958 (Special Projects Office 1958). Its original intent was twofold: to simulate the logic of a new project taking the form of a flow diagram to manage schedules, and to assess the statistical probability of actually achieving the plan.

As introduced, PERT had a strong emphasis on statistical probability, which constituted one of the early difficulties. At the time (in the late 1950s), neither computers nor computer software programs were available to adequately implement the concept. Nevertheless, PERT as a tool caught the imagination of both management practitioners and academia members.

PERT as a scheduling technique was not as successful as the critical path method that came along at about the same time, but in another industry. Two men working with these concepts described the events at the time:

In 1956, E. I. DuPont de Nemours undertook a thorough investigation of the extent to which a computer might be used to improve the planning and scheduling, rescheduling, and progress reporting of the company's engineering programs. A DuPont engineer, Morgan R. Walker, and a Remington-Rand computer expert, James E. Kelley Jr., worked on the problem, and in late 1957 ran a pilot test of a system using a unique arrow-diagram or network method which came to be known as the Critical Path Method (Archibald and Villoria 1967).

In about 1962, the advocates of PERT as a scheduling tool chose to take another bold step to broaden the concept. Their thinking: If one could accurately simulate the logic of a project taking the form of a network, why not add resources into the network and manage both time and costs? The result was the introduction of PERT/cost in 1962. To accurately describe this experiment at the time, since neither the computer hardware nor computer software programs were available to properly support network scheduling, the addition of cost resources to these logic networks merely exacerbated the problem.

Neither the original PERT (which then went by the term "PERT/time") nor PERT/cost survived by the mid-1960s. Today, the term "PERT" does live on, but only used as a generic term to describe any scheduling network. In fact, most of the networks today that are called PERT are actually precedence diagram method networks, not true PERT networks.

What of importance did survive from the short-lived PERT/cost experience was the earned value concept. The implementation of PERT/cost to industry at the time required eleven reporting formats from the contractors. One of these formats included a "cost of work report." Its format had what was called the "value of work performed" versus the actual costs:

A comparison of the actual costs accumulated to date and the contract estimate for the work performed to date will show whether the work is being performed at a cost which is greater or less than planned (Office of the Secretary of Defense and National Aeronautics and Space Administration 1962).

Earned value as a project management tool was thus first formally introduced to modern industry in 1962. As a part of PERT/cost, however, it would not last long. PERT/cost had a lifespan of perhaps three years; but it did leave an important legacy: the use of earned value data to monitor the true cost performance during the life of a project.

By the mid-1960s, both PERT and PERT/cost had all but vanished from the scene. Industry executives and private companies did not take kindly to being told what management techniques they must employ and how they must manage their projects, no matter how useful such ideas may be. The DOD project managers had to take a more sensitive approach toward private industry; they did just that with the C/SCSC criteria approach.

Phase 2—C/SCSC: 1967 to 1996

The U.S. Air Force (USAF) took the lead in the initiative to set standards that would allow it to oversee contractors' performance. In 1965, the USAF formed a team called the Cost Schedule Planning and Control Specification group, and meetings were held by some of the very same people who had been involved in the earlier implementation of PERT/time and PERT/cost. By virtue of their PERT experience, they quickly agreed that they would not impose any specific "management control system" on industry. Rather, they conceived the notion of merely requiring that contractors satisfy defined "criteria" with their existing management control systems. A subtle difference from the PERT experience, but it made all the difference between success and failure for the new concept.

The criteria approach simply required a response from industry to some rather basic questions, but based on sound project management principles. One individual, who was a part of this process, described what he hoped to ascertain:

> Does the contractor break down the work into short span packages that can be budgeted, scheduled, and evaluated? Do they have a cost accumulation system? Do they measure performance against those packages of work ... and do they then report status and variances to their own internal management? We don't want to tell anyone how to manage (Driessnack 1990).

By December 1967, DOD was ready to formally issue what it called its Cost/Schedule Control Systems Criteria, shortened to simply C/SCSC. The C/SCSC carefully incorporated the earned value concept in the form of thirty-five criteria that were imposed on any contractor wishing to be selected for any new major systems contract or subcontract over a certain funding threshold. The DOD imposed these thirty-five criteria on a contractor's management control system anytime that a cost or incentive-type contract was used.

Over the three decades since these criteria have been in place, the practitioners of the concept have developed a significant amount of scientific knowledge, based on the employment of these standards. Much knowledge has been gathered on earned value, both scientific and simply empirical. These findings will be covered in our next chapter.

However, the concept of earned value within the C/SCSC has been largely restricted to the acquisition of major systems by governments. Private industry, with but a few exceptions, has not completely embraced the full and formal criteria concept.

Earned value within the C/SCSC produced mixed results. The utilization of the EVM within the C/SCSC provided some impressive results. But in other cases, the experience has been less than satisfactory from private industry's perspective. One of the positive aspects was the resulting body of scientific knowledge based on actual experiences with hundreds of projects. But there have also been some negative experiences, and we should candidly discuss those experiences as well, so as to not repeat them in the future.

The C/SCSC went through some three decades of bureaucratic interpretations that distanced them from the original objectives set forth in 1966 when the criteria were first defined. These esoteric interpretations subsequently led to the preparation of formal (rigid) implementation guides, surveillance manuals, and implementation checklists containing over a hundred (174) questions for the use of the practitioners. The checklists themselves became absolute litmus tests used to impose additional requirements on contractor's management control systems. In some cases, there have been reasonable applications of the checklists. But in other cases, the applications have been, shall we say, somewhat arbitrary and perhaps even dogmatic.

The checklist questions were intended by the originators to be used as a guideline only, to be exercised with professional judgment. However, it would seem that some practitioners had elevated their checklists and associated questions to a position on par with the original thirty-five criteria. Contractors do understand the importance of having to meet certain standards, but resisted many of the minor peripheral issues that were raised as absolute requirements.

A sort of cultist society of C/SCSC professional practitioners emerged, which did not sit well with many (most) of the project managers in the private sector. Project managers look for simple tools that will assist them in meeting their primary mission of completing their projects on time, within the authorized funds, while achieving all of the technical objectives.

C/SCSC was a success from a government perspective, because it permitted the oversight of contractor performance whenever the risks of cost growth rest squarely with the government. Applications with the government have been consistent and have met the test of time, and the original thirty-five criteria remained consistent and unchanged.

However, earned value as contained in the original C/SCSC was never accepted or adopted by private industry in the management of its internal projects. And there were valid reasons for this outright rejection.

A new foreign language emerged. Perhaps the single most difficult aspect associated with C/SCSC for project managers in the private sector was the need to accept the terminology associated with the formal doctrine. Did the earned value concept need to be this complicated? We think not.

For example, instead of calling a plan a "plan," or the "planned value," C/SCSC practitioners chose the term "Budgeted Cost for Work Scheduled," or "BCWS," or sometimes simply "S." Instead of using the term "earned value," or "earned standards," which would suggest physical accomplishments, the term "Budgeted Cost of Work Performed," or "BCWP," or simply "P" was used. Skilled project managers do not typically respond to terms like "S" or "P," and they do object to having to learn a new cryptic vocabulary.

Perhaps one of the more interesting and unexplainable phenomena in the usage of terms for C/SCSC applications was in the deliberate avoidance of ever using the dreaded word "overrun." Interestingly, the avoidance of cost overruns was the primary reason why EVM was being required on projects in the first place. But instead of calling an overrun an "overrun," such incomprehensible terms as "OTB," which stood for "over target baseline," "formal reprogramming," or "variance at completion" were substituted for the more unambiguous terms.

Phase 3—EVM (ANSI/EIA 748): 1996 to Present

In spite of the impressive results with the use of earned value within the C/SCSC, there was concern from both within private industry and the U.S. government, its DOD, that earned value had to be made more "user friendly" if the concept was to be applied beyond a government mandate.

On 18 April 1995 in Phoenix, Arizona, at a formal meeting of the Management Systems Subcommittee of the National Defense Industrial Association (NDIA), that group took on the task of reviewing and possibly rewriting the DOD's formal earned value criteria. Its objective: to make the criteria more compatible with the needs of private industry.

Over the next few months, members of the subcommittee met, discussed, and established their own version of the thirty-five C/SCSC. They called the industry version the Earned Value Management System (EVMS) criteria, and it contained just thirty-two criteria, each of them rewritten in a simpler form. Gone were the vague terms of BCWS and BCWP, and in their place were put "planned value" and "earned value." It was an attempt to make earned value more useful as a tool for project managers to use.

Then on 14 December 1996, the Under Secretary of Defense for Acquisition and Technology, Dr. Paul Kaminski, accepted verbatim the thirty-two industry earned value criteria. The thirty-two EVMS criteria were later incorporated into the next revision of the DOD Instruction 5000.2R in early 1997.

The Management Systems Subcommittee of the NDIA was not content to simply have EVM restricted to the DOD. The NDIA subcommittee then requested and obtained approval for these thirty-two EVM criteria to be formally issued as an American National Standard Institute/Electronic Industry Association (ANSI/EIA) document. In July 1998, the ANSI/EIA 748 Guide was officially issued.

The significance of these moves does not lie in the revised wording of the criteria, or in the minimal reduction in their number from thirty-five to thirty-two. Rather, the important change was in the attitude of all parties to the process. During 1997, there was a sort of changing of the EVMS responsibility from that of a government mandate into ownership of EVM by private industry. Private industry was adopting the EVM technique not because it was a government requirement, but because it represented a viable, best-practice tool, that project managers everywhere could use.

(**Note**: There are two appendices to this book that deal with the full EVM criteria. Appendix I contains the author's unofficial description of each of the thirty-two EVM criteria. Appendix II provides a comparison of the original thirty-five C/SCSC criteria with the reworded thirty-two EVM criteria.)

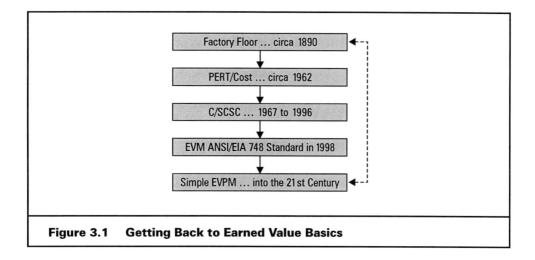

Figure 3.1   Getting Back to Earned Value Basics

In Summary

Although many positive steps have been taken recently to make the earned value concept more user friendly, much remains to be done. We have the opportunity to make earned value into a widely accepted tool for broad-based project management applications. But we must go back to the simple basics.

Shown in Figure 3.1 is a chart that depicts the evolution of the earned value concept. It all started in the factories over a hundred years ago. The industrial engineers who conceived the concept used it as a simple management tool. We in private industry should now do likewise.

We suggest a return to the original approach used by industrial engineers, but while incorporating the critical success results from applications of the formal C/SCSC and EVM. Use a simple form of earned value to manage all projects within the private sector.

Chapter 4

The Earned Value
Body of Knowledge

In somewhat the same manner that the Project Management Institute (PMI®) has carefully documented the empirical evidence on the profession of project management, which has resulted in the creation and publication of *A Guide to the Project Management Body of Knowledge (PMBOK® Guide)*, there has been a similar but less formal accumulation of data on the subject of Earned Value Management (EVM). Most of the data has been gathered by practitioners operating within the United States (U.S.) Department of Defense (DOD) community. While the concept of earned value began with the industrial engineers in the factories at the turn of the last century, the actual collection of knowledge centered on its practical project applications has been done over the past three decades.

Since implementing earned value as an integral part of the Cost/ Schedule Control Systems Criteria (C/SCSC) in 1967, the criteria concept has been consistently applied to major new development projects. There have been no substitutive changes in the earned value criteria for over thirty years. Therefore, the analysis of the findings and the conclusions reached can reasonably be considered to be valid empirical doctrine. These accumulated findings have evolved into what is fast becoming an embryonic EVM science.

In particular, performance management personnel within the Office of the Under Secretary of Defense for Acquisitions has been responsible for the scientific analyses of several hundred contract applications where the earned value criteria have been employed. It has formulated some rather sophisticated scientific conclusions based on the consistency, predictability, and reliability of the earned value data. Its findings should not be ignored by those managing projects in the private sector. Quite possibly, project managers in the private sector will discover another valuable tool for their use in the management of all projects.

The DOD effort has been augmented by studies done at the Air Force Institute of Technology (AFIT) in Dayton, Ohio, which has expanded the empirical observations on this evolving management science. It might be beneficial also to review some of these findings to see if they might apply to more universal applications to all projects ... yes, even in the private sector.

The Legacy of Earned Value As a Part of the C/SCSC

For a number of years, we have been following the achievements made by those who have championed earned value as it has been a part of the C/SCSC. The findings and knowledge that they have accumulated are truly impressive. Far too often the focus has been on the negative aspects of the C/SCSC, frequently centering on the sometimes-overzealous government practitioners who have carried their demands on private sector contractors to the extreme.

Nevertheless, the good aspects of earned value far outweigh the negative. And the recent trend within the U.S. government has been toward giving more latitude to private contractors to employ those practices that are most comfortable for them. We would like now to focus on the body of knowledge that has been accumulated by individuals within the Pentagon and the individual branches of the military services.

If it would even be possible, it would likely take months or possibly years to coordinate a collective position as to which are the more significant achievements resulting from the employment of earned value since the C/SCSC were first introduced nearly three decades ago. Therefore, we have not attempted to reach any type of broad popular consensus.

Rather, we have assembled our own listing of just ten items of what we feel have been the most important accomplishments resulting from the employment of earned value. These ten findings, to us, constitute the early beginnings of an earned value body of knowledge.

1. The employment of a single management control system that will provide accurate, consistent, reliable, and timely data to management at all levels, allowing it to monitor the performance of all projects or production work within an enterprise.

One of the primary benefits of employing earned value is that it allows for the use of a single management approach that can be applied to both projects and production work within any given organization. The relationship of what work was scheduled versus what work was accomplished provides an accurate indicator of whether or not one is meeting the time expectations of management. Also, the relationship of what work was accomplished versus how much money was spent to accomplish the work provides an accurate reflection of the true cost performance.

Far too often, companies will employ multiple management-control systems to monitor activities. One approach may be used to monitor the work on big projects, another for the smaller projects, and still another used to oversee the production work, and so forth. Earned value data is somewhat analogous to measuring the temperature of the human body. If the human body temperature is higher or lower than the standard of 98.6 degrees, the doctor will know to look further. Likewise, earned value data penetrating set parameters must be examined by management. Earned value data is consistent for all projects and production work within the enterprise.

By employing a single management system on all activities within an enterprise, the temptation to put a positive spin on negative results will be minimized. Sometimes in the past, companies have allowed their various managers to take different interpretations of the same actual results. The project manager, executive management, functional management, chief financial officer, and others would interpret the same performance results to reinforce their own parochial positions. Often, one person's interpretation would not match another's interpretation of the same results. One set of books, reflecting accurate data, is possible when employing EVM.

2. A management approach that requires the integration of the technical scope of work with the time commitments and the authorized resources, thus allowing for the measurement of integrated performance throughout the life of a project or a production run.

While most management theorists will be quick to express support for any approach that integrates the work to de done with the necessary time and resources, rarely in practice does such integration actually happen. Typically, the contract administrators will define a project in one way, the technical specialists in another, and the resource estimators will view the same requirements in still a different way. The scheduling community, not to be outdone, has always had its own unique perspective of what is important, which may be different from what others have determined. The result: any given project will often be implemented by the sum of various parochial and conflicting interests. Each function may well measure and report on its own performance in a manner that is in conflict with other functional tracking metrics. Whether or not we like it, most projects are defined and then performed in a nonintegrated manner.

Sometime in the early 1960s came a concept called the Work Breakdown Structure (WBS). The WBS provided an opportunity for all key functions on a given project to view the project in a like manner, to speak with a common project language for the first time. Collectively, all key functions would have the opportunity to define a given project in a like manner, which would then relate to other functional perspectives.

With use of a WBS, key functions would now be expected to decompose a project into progressively smaller units, down to the work-task level, at which point they would relate the technical work to be done, the estimated resources needed, and the time frame for each task. With use of the WBS, all critical functions would be expected to work within an integrated project plan. Performance could be measured at the lowest task level, allowing the project manager to ascertain how much work had been planned, how much work was accomplished, and how much money has been spent to accomplish the work. The use of a WBS allowed for performance measurement to take place in an integrated manner.

Shown in Figure 4.1 is a comparison of these two management approaches. On the left side is the more traditional functional matrix approach, which most projects have employed. Here, each of the various functions will take its own peculiar interpretation of project requirements, according to its own unique perspective. This approach encouraged projects to be implemented in a nonintegrated manner.

By contrast, on the right side of Figure 4.1 is an integrated management approach, required in order to employ EVM. Each function must work in concert with all other functions on the same defined work, all within the project's WBS. Multifunctional work is defined, authorized, performed, and reported within management control points, typically called Control Account Plans, or CAPs. Each management control point or CAP will be placed at the lowest element within the WBS. The WBS has thus provided the vehicle for the integration of all project and production work.

3. Documented empirical evidence collected from over 700 DOD contracts that have employed earned value management ... reflecting a pattern of consistent and predictable performance history (Beach 1990).

Since the mid-1970s, the performance management practitioners within the DOD have been empirically tracking the actual results of all contracts that have employed EVM as an integral part of the C/SCSC criteria.

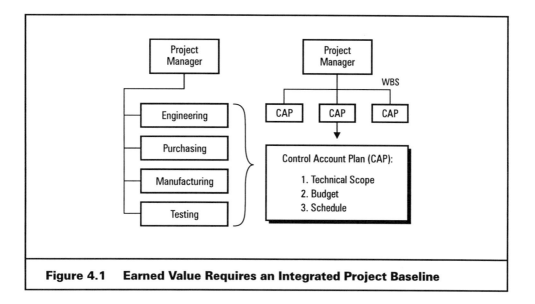

Figure 4.1   Earned Value Requires an Integrated Project Baseline

They have documented their findings, analyzed the results, and hypothesized final performance patterns for contracts that employ earned value.

These findings have been spectacular in that they have demonstrated a pattern of predictable project performance that can be used to scientifically forecast the future. See Figure 4.2 for the summary results of these findings. This same chart initially was prepared by DOD practitioners in the early 1980s, with only the sample of contracts changing, from originally 100 projects to now well over 700 projects. Most impressive empirical findings.

Their hypothesis: as early as the 15 percent completion point in a project, the actual performance results (the earned value efficiencies), can be used as an "early warning" indicator to management. Such results can be used to predict the final costs and time requirements within a predictable (finite) range of values. The results of work accomplished against a given plan can be used to forecast the final project or production results. Their empirical conclusions are simple: If a project has overrun the work it has accomplished to date, that overrun will not be recovered on the remaining work. In fact, they conclude that overruns typically tend to get progressively worse, not better, with time.

Without attempting to explain the reasons for these conclusions, DOD practitioners suggest that there is a natural tendency for any project team to do its best scope definition, planning, scheduling, estimating, and so on for the near-term work. And as the project extends into later periods, things like scope, schedule, and budget will be progressively more vague,

---

GIVEN:
Contract more than 15% complete
  1. Overrun at completion will not be less than overrun to date.
  2. Percent overrun at completion will be greater than percent overrun to date.

CONCLUSION:
You can't recover!

WHO SAYS:
More than 700 major DOD contracts since 1977.

WHY:
If you underestimated the near, then there is no hope that you did better on the far-term planning.

Figure 4.2   The DOD Earned Value Body of Knowledge

more imperfect. Thus, future performance trends likely will deteriorate as the project continues to its completion.

4. The utility and stability of the cumulative Cost Performance Index [CPI(e)], that delicate relationship between the physical work actually accomplished versus the costs spent to perform such work to continuously monitor the performance trends of a project.

As early as the 15 to 20 percent completion point of any project, the cumulative cost performance efficiency factors (earned values versus costs) have been demonstrated to be stable, and the data provided can be used to predict the final range of costs for any given project. This index is referred to as the CPI(e), with the "e" representing the cost efficiency.

(**Note of Caution**: These same forecasting results are not possible with periodic or incremental performance data, which have been found to experience wide fluctuations. Periodic performance data thus have limited utility as a long-term trending tool. But periodic data are obviously needed to continuously monitor the most immediate results on a project. Only cumulative data is valid for predicting the final performance results.)

Individuals at the U.S. AFIT have been instrumental in extending the scientific knowledge begun in the Pentagon. One significant study provided insight into these findings:

Using data from a sample of completed Air Force contracts, Christensen/Payne established that the cumulative CPI did not change by more than 10 percent from the value at the 20 percent contract completion point.

Based on data from the Defense Acquisition Executive Summary (DAES) database, results indicate that the cumulative CPI is stable from the 20 percent completion point regardless of contract type, program, or service.

Knowing that the cumulative CPI is important, the government can now conclude that a contractor is in serious trouble when it overruns the budget beyond the 20 percent completion point (Christensen and Heise 1993, 7, 13).

Let us reflect on these empirical findings. No longer must management wait until all the funds have been spent to determine that additional budget will be needed in order to complete the full scope of a given project. This is the project manager's "early warning signal," and perhaps the most compelling reason why any project should employ some form of earned value.

By monitoring cumulative cost performance against a detailed project plan, and by relating the value of the work performed against the costs of doing that work, a predictable pattern becomes available to management early in the life cycle of the project. Such patterns can be used by management to both assess the performance to date and to predict the final performance results.

The CPI (based on cost efficiency) is determined by dividing the value of the work actually performed (the earned value) by the actual costs that it took to accomplish the earned value. The use of the cumulative CPI(e) is displayed in Figure 4.3. Perfect cost performance is 1.0. Less than 1.0 performance reflects the condition typically called "overrun."

One more point needs to be made on the utility of the cumulative CPI for universal project management. The earlier findings reflect data produced by major DOD acquisition projects. A major project will take months to establish a baseline against which performance can be measured, and, thus, the CPI results known.

But how about the typical smaller projects of perhaps only one year's duration? Such projects can be defined and planned with a performance measurement baseline before go-ahead by management. Such projects can have their performance measured from the start of the project. Thus, accurate cumulative CPI readings could become available as early as perhaps 10 percent into the life cycle of any project, which is employing a simple form of earned value measurement.

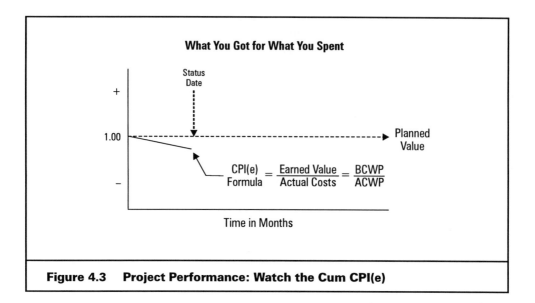

What You Got for What You Spent

Status
Date

+

1.00 - ➤ Planned
Value

$$CPI(e) \atop Formula = {Earned\ Value \over Actual\ Costs} = {BCWP \over ACWP}$$

−

Time in Months

Figure 4.3   Project Performance: Watch the Cum CPI(e)

5. The utility of the Schedule Performance Index (SPI), that delicate relationship between the physical work actually accomplished versus the work initially scheduled, in order to monitor and manage the schedule to completion.

One of the more important benefits of employing a performance measurement system is to be able to determine how much of the originally scheduled work has been physically accomplished at any point in time. The issue is fundamental: is the project on its schedule, ahead of schedule, or behind the work scheduled to do? And if there are differences in the schedule performance, what is the value of such work?

Such schedule performance knowledge is particularly powerful for any project when it is compared against the project's critical path position. Both the SPI and critical path method indicators, when used in concert, will accurately assess the true schedule position of any project.

Even though the SPI may have little relationship to the project's critical path, falling behind in accomplishing the work scheduled is one of the early indicators of potential future problems. Project managers do not like to get behind in their scheduled work, even though perhaps a more important indicator will be the results against the project's critical path.

The natural tendency when one falls behind the planned work is to add unplanned resources in an attempt to catch up, effectively to do the same work as was planned, but by spending more money to accomplish the same effort. Arbitrary decisions to catch up on the planned work, to improve the SPI performance, can cause nonrecoverable damage to the project's cost performance. The SPI is a useful schedule monitoring indicator that should be used in conjunction with critical path methodology.

The SPI is determined by dividing the value of the work performed (the earned value) by the value of the work planned to be accomplished (the planned value) as of any point in time. It is a valuable indicator and can be used with the CPI(e) to predict the final required project costs.

6. The utility of the cumulative CPI(e) to statistically forecast the "low-end" range of final estimated costs at completion.

The cumulative CPI(e) has been scientifically shown to be a stable indicator of project performance. Perhaps its most significant utility is the ability to use the cumulative CPI(e) to statistically forecast the final cost requirements for any project.

A statistical forecast of the total funds required may be done by simply taking the project work remaining (total project budget less the earned value achieved), dividing this value by the cumulative CPI(e), and then adding the actual costs spent. This formula provides what some consider the "best case" or a "low-end" forecast for a project within a statistical range of final cost estimates.

7. The utility of the cumulative CPI(e) when used in conjunction with the cumulative SPI to statistically forecast the "high-end" range of final estimated costs at completion.

The combination of the cumulative CPI(e) when used in conjunction with the cumulative SPI provides the ability to also statistically forecast the final cost results of a project. Some consider this technique to represent the "most likely" or the "high end" in the range of statistical possibilities.

The rationale for this combination: if a project is both behind its planned schedule position and is overrunning its costs to date, these two conditions will combine to exacerbate the final results. The use of the CPI(e) alone and the CPI(e) with the SPI as forecasting tools will be discussed in detail in a later chapter on forecasting the final cost results.

8. The utility of the To Complete Performance Index (TCPI) to monitor the remaining project work against specific management financial goals.

The remaining (to-go) project work constitutes the only area where a project manager can influence the final cost results. Costs already spent or committed are effectively "sunk costs," nonrecoverable costs. Therefore, it is useful to any project to determine what performance factors it will take to accomplish the remaining effort in order to achieve a specific management objective. Such management goals can be variable and can reflect the original project budget, or, if actual results so dictate, can also represent an increased financial goal, reflecting a more realistic and attainable objective.

The TCPI focuses on the remaining project tasks. It is effectively the mirror opposite of the cumulative CPI(e) in that it reflects what it will take to recover from a negative actual cost performance position.

The TCPI takes the work remaining (the total budget less the earned value accomplished) and divides it by the funds remaining (the latest management financial goal less funds spent) to determine what performance results it will take to meet such goals. The TCPI can be an effective indicator for management at all levels to monitor the remaining project tasks. More will be covered on this subject in a later chapter.

9. The utility of a weekly (or periodic) Cost Performance Index [CPI(p)] to monitor performance results for production or repetitive-type work.

Although the use of cumulative data has been found to work well to determine the long-term trend or direction of a project, industrial engineers monitoring production work have used periodic or weekly data to track the cost performance achieved against an established production standard. By breaking down a total production effort into detailed subassemblies, and then establishing a weekly production standard (a planned value) for each assembly, the tracking of production effort has been successfully employed with use of what is called a CPI(p).

The CPI(p) refers to "performance," and the formula is the opposite of the more widely used CPI(e). It is determined by dividing the actual costs incurred to accomplish the earned value by the value of the physical work performed (earned value) during the measured or incremental period. Displayed in Figure 4.4 is an example of the CPI(p) plotted weekly against the established equivalent unit costs for a given manufactured part, component, or assembly.

Compare the two earned value indices displayed in Figure 4.3, a project cost efficiency CPI(e), with Figure 4.4, a weekly production CPI(p), against an industrial standard.

10. The use of Management by Exception (MBE) principles to focus management's attention on the significant exceptions to an authorized plan, allowing management to effectively monitor the critical aspects of performance and then to develop and apply timely corrective actions.

Lastly—and perhaps the ultimate utility in the use of earned value performance measurement—is that it allows for the employment of the MBE principles against an established and authorized project or production

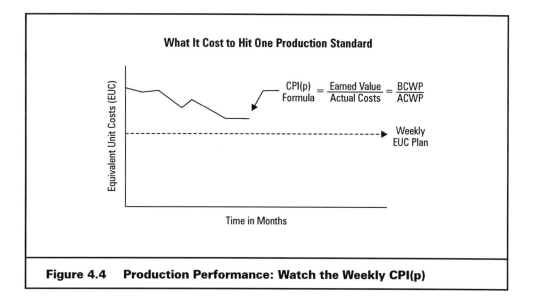

Figure 4.4   Production Performance: Watch the Weekly CPI(p)

baseline plan. With EVM, management need not follow each and every detailed task in order to effectively oversee the performance of authorized work. Rather, by focusing on only those exceptions to the authorized plans in accordance with specified variance thresholds, management can effectively monitor all critical aspects of performance against the project or production plan.

These ten items represent to us the more significant findings of the body of knowledge that has resulted from over three decades in the employment of EVM. We will use these findings as a basis to suggest a simplified form of the earned value for use with the other more-established project and production management tools. What we hope to achieve is a simple form of earned value, a "poor-person's" earned value, for use on all projects and production work, of any size, and in any industry.

Chapter 5

Scope the Project

There likely is no factor that would contribute more to the success of any project than having a good and complete definition of the project's scope of work. Conversely, there is probably no factor that would contribute more quickly to the demise of any project than to initiate a new endeavor without understanding the full scope of work. Interestingly, the earned value technique cannot be employed on any project unless the project manager has defined the total job. Scope creep, if allowed to happen, would negate the ability to accurately measure project performance.

Understanding the Job (What's In ... What's Out)

Planning a new project that employs Earned Value Performance Measurement (EVPM) is no different than the initial planning necessary to implement any project. It always helps to know what makes up the project, the whole project, and particularly the outer limits of the project. We can think of at least three reasons why this is important to project managers.

First, you need to know when the project is over. You need to know when all the work that you originally set out to do has been done. You need to have a tangible metric for any project called "done." You need to know when you may start work on the next project.

Second, you need to know the difference between agreed-to work and new work requests—that is, whenever someone brings in more work for you to do than you had originally agreed to do. For example, if you agree to peel ten baskets of potatoes, and someone brings in an eleventh basket, then you will want to ask for additional compensation (an adjustment in the project's price) for doing that eleventh basket. Unless you sufficiently defined the work in the first place, you may not be able to tell the difference between basket ten, eleven, twelve, and so on.

Third—and perhaps this is most critical to the earned value cost management concept—you will need to know how much of the entire job has been accomplished ... at any point in time. The issue is fundamental: If you do not know what constitutes 100 percent of a project, how will you ever know if you are 10, 50, or 90 percent done? You must know what constitutes 100 percent of the project scope in order to tell how much of it you have performed during the life of the project. The Project Management Institute's (PMI) Olde Curmudgeon (an anonymously written column in *PM Network* magazine) stated this issue well years ago:

> Failure to define what is a part of the project, as well as what is not, may result in work being performed that was unnecessary to create the product of the project and thus lead to both schedule and budget overruns (Olde Curmudgeon 1994).

In Chapter 5 of *A Guide to the Project Management Body of Knowledge (PMBOK® Guide)*, scope management is addressed. The chapter's opening paragraph describes well the importance of any project knowing what it has agreed to do, and, perhaps of greater importance, knowing what it has not agreed to do, which it calls the project boundaries:

> Project Scope Management includes the processes required to ensure that the project includes all the work required, and only the work required, to complete the project successfully. It is primarily concerned with defining and controlling what is or is not included in the project (PMI Standards Committee 1996, 47).

One of the key pillars of the earned value concept is that the project manager must know at all times what percentage of the physical work has been accomplished, the percent complete, as related to the total job. This information is needed in order to compare the physical work done against the actual costs spent to perform that work in the same measured period. The relationship between the total physical work accomplished as compared to the total dollars spent provides the answer to: "What did we get for the dollars we spent?" For example, if you spent 30 percent of the project's total budget and accomplished only 25 percent of the total project's physical work, then what do you call this condition? Answer: *a 20 percent overrun!*

A Work Breakdown Structure to Scope the Project

Starting sometime in the early 1960s, there developed a school of thought centered on the belief that project managers needed a new device, a tool similar in utility to the company organizational chart. For years, corporate executives have been using their organizational charts to conceptually define in graphical form: 1) who does what in the company, 2) who is responsible for what, and 3) who reports to whom within their organization.

This notion that project managers needed a special tool led to the creation of the Work Breakdown Structure (WBS). The WBS is to the project manager what the organizational chart is to the company executive.

The WBS is a tool that is used by the project manager to define a project and give it cohesiveness so that the project can be managed as a one-time unique effort, a transient unit of work passing through the firm's permanent organization. At any point in time, a given company will have many projects in work, each competing with each other for limited company resources. The WBS is the device that integrates the project effort and sets one project apart from all other projects within the same organization.

(**An important point often missed by some**: Although the WBS looks like an organizational chart, it definitely is not an organizational chart. Unfortunately, however, the WBS does look much like an organizational chart. Some people get confused about this issue and draw a project organizational chart that they then label as their WBS. This is wrong. The project WBS is not the project's organization chart, but the WBS can be used to first define and then assign project work.)

An example of a project WBS is shown in Figure 5.1, representing a diagram for a United States Department of Energy (DOE) project. Note that this is a "product"-oriented hierarchy that progressively breaks out the work elements downward from the top WBS box, called WBS level 1.

The owner of a project will frequently specify that the top three levels of the "project WBS" define the reporting requirements. Then the performing project manager will extend the "contract WBS" down to lower levels to assist in the management of the project by integrating the technical work, costs, and schedule. A key point is that the WBS must reflect how the project manager plans to manage the project. Much early thought by both the owner and the performing project manager must be given to the WBS.

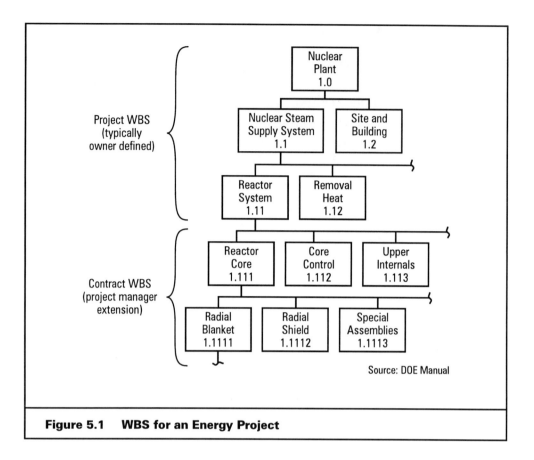

Figure 5.1   WBS for an Energy Project

The emphasis for the WBS must be on the project, project tasks, unique work to be done to accomplish the project objectives, and deliverables. Some of the key words that should be a part of any viable WBS definition would be: "project end-items," "project deliverables," "project tasks" and "project subtasks."

One of the best definitions of the WBS was published in 1976 in which the author was describing what he called at the time a Project Breakdown Structure (PBS). In retrospect, the term "PBS" is perhaps a more descriptive term than WBS. However the term "WBS" stuck, and PBS did not:

> The PBS is a graphic portrayal of the project, exploding it in a level-by-level fashion, down to the degree of detail needed for effective planning and control. It must include all deliverable end items ... and include the major functional tasks that must be performed. ... (Archibald 1976).

The PBS would appear to have its primary focus on the product, whereas the WBS has its focus on the project's work tasks. Since most of the project managers of the world and the *PMBOK® Guide* use the term "WBS," we will do likewise.

The *PMBOK® Guide* definition of a WBS is also quite informative and perhaps worthy of our review. It defines a WBS as:

> a deliverable-oriented grouping of project elements that organizes and defines the total scope of the project: work not in the WBS is outside the scope of the project. As with the scope statement, the WBS is often used to develop or confirm a common understanding of project scope. Each descending level represents an increasingly detailed description of the project elements (PMI Standards Committee 1996, 54).

By essentially forcing the project team to define its necessary work tasks into progressively greater detail with the use of a WBS, the total scope of the project will then take form. The WBS in total will define what is inside and what is outside of any given project. Returning once again to remarks made by PMI's cranky Olde Curmudgeon:

> A project consists of the sum total of all the elements of the WBS. Conversely, an element that is not contained in the WBS is not a part of the project. Any work that cannot be identified in the WBS requires authorization to proceed, either as a recognized omission or as an approved change order (Olde Curmudgeon 1994).

At the lowest WBS element, a project will want to expand the brief task labels into a descriptive narrative that can then evolve into what is referred to as the WBS dictionary. The WBS dictionary in total will typically comprise the project's technical statement of work (SOW). The WBS dictionary may also be used to relate the defined work tasks directly to specific organizational units who will perform the actual work, likely in some form of a project-matrix organization. The project's contractual specialists will also have use for the WBS dictionary to serve as the basis for creating the contractual SOW between the owner and the project manager.

Illustrated in Figure 5.2 is an imaginary WBS for the World War II Manhattan Project managed by perhaps the ultimate in project managers, Lieutenant General Leslie R. Groves. While the Manhattan Project took place before the introduction of the WBS concept, as any good project manager would, General Groves likely envisioned this type of subdivision of the work to be done. The point we want to emphasize is that the WBS provides an excellent vehicle for achieving a complete definition of project scope. When a narrative description is added to each WBS element, the WBS dictionary, in essence, becomes the project's official SOW.

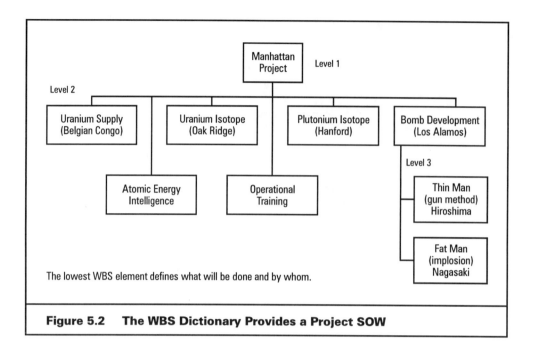

Figure 5.2   The WBS Dictionary Provides a Project SOW

By starting with the complete project definition in the form of a WBS, and with a buy-in by all key functional organizations, any project will have better assurances that the work being done will represent what the customer desires.

Some Specific Examples of WBSs

Perhaps the best way to illustrate the utility of the WBS is with a review of some specific examples. Shown in Figure 5.1 is a WBS for an energy project. This illustrates a product-type breakout, exploding the project from the top down into progressively smaller units.

By way of contrast, an energy project is shown in Figure 5.3, but this time for a construction job. In this case, the WBS reflects the critical phases of the construction effort and the manner in which the project manager plans to manage the effort.

The design work likely will be sent to an outside company, as indicated in the box designated "Design 1.1" in Figure 5.3. The project team will procure the expensive and/or common materials to achieve a cost savings, as indicated in the box designated "Procurement 1.2." The actual construction effort will be contracted to still another firm, as reflected in the box labeled "Construction 1.3." In this case, the WBS reflects how the

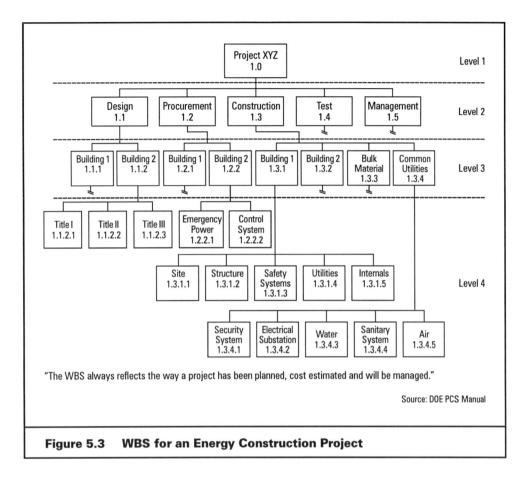

"The WBS always reflects the way a project has been planned, cost estimated and will be managed."

Source: DOE PCS Manual

Figure 5.3   WBS for an Energy Construction Project

major project effort will be managed at level 2: "Design," "Procurement," and "Construction."

Figure 5.3 is a chart taken from the DOE Project Control System (PCS), and a key point is contained in the quote from its PCS Manual, as shown at the bottom of Figure 5.3: "The WBS always reflects the way a project has been planned, cost estimated and will be managed." A key point is that the WBS must be owned by the project manager and the project management team, and reflect the way that they plan to perform the effort. The WBS should not be the property of any single function, although all functions working on the project must have a say in its formation and buy-in to the final WBS. However, the WBS must ultimately be the exclusive property of the project manager, used to define the project.

Continuing with specific examples of WBSs, the Department of Defense (DOD) took the lead in the mid-1960s in defining a WBS standard for its industry. This was both good and frankly bad for project management. The DOD's WBS document was then called Military Standard

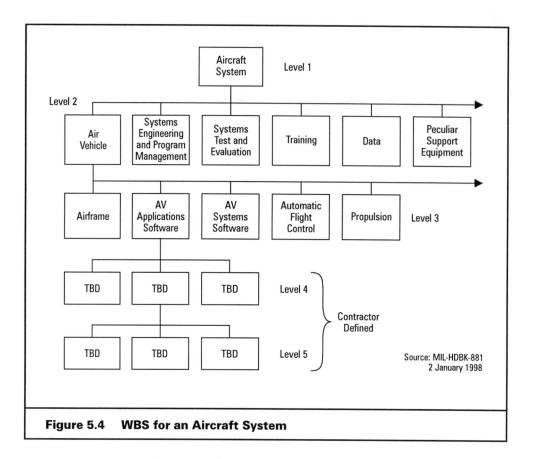

Figure 5.4   WBS for an Aircraft System

881 (MIL-STD 881), and it specified in very specific terms the format in which the WBS was to be used. MIL-STD 881 defined seven specific systems to be managed: aircraft, electronic, missile, ordnance, ship, space, and surface vehicles. Interestingly, at least three of our more popular project challenges (opportunities) today are missing from this listing of seven systems: construction, environmental clean-up, and software projects.

Shown in Figure 5.4 is an example of one of the seven specific DOD WBS formats, this one covering an aircraft system. Level two of any WBS is most critical, because at level two the project manager will indicate the approach planned to manage the project. With MIL-STD 881, the particular system would be displayed to the extreme left of level two, then a series of common elements would be listed from left to right. MIL-STD 881 was very specific in defining the remainder of the authorized elements allowed at WBS level two: systems engineering and project management, system test and evaluation, training, data, peculiar support equipment, common support equipment, operational site activation, industrial facilities, and spares/repair parts.

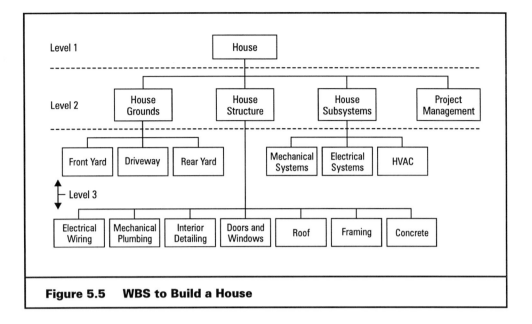

Figure 5.5   WBS to Build a House

There was nothing unreasonable or anti-project management contained in these nine common elements, as precisely specified in the DOD MIL-STD 881. However, project managers are unique individuals who do not take kindly to being told by anyone how they must define or manage their projects. Considerable friction emerged over the years between the project managers and the government buyers when the project managers were told that they must structure their project WBSs to conform to the specific breakouts contained in this military standard. The DOD's standard WBS encroached on the creative territory of project managers, and they resented this intrusion.

We are fortunate today to have the use of relational databases and project management software coding sufficient to make these earlier WBS problems somewhat of a non-issue. The principle that should guide us is that the WBS belongs to the project manager, and the WBS should represent the way that the project manager plans to manage the project ... period.

Illustrated in Figure 5.5 is a simple WBS to build a house. In this case, the project manager is planning to divide the project into three distinct categories to manage, as shown at level two of the WBS: grounds, structure, and subsystems. All other categories of the project will be lumped into the general category to the extreme right, called project management, which might also include such important activities as design, financing, obtaining building permits, and so on.

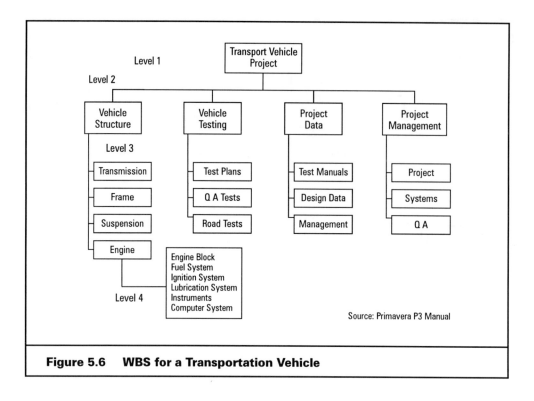

Figure 5.6   WBS for a Transportation Vehicle

Another WBS example is shown in Figure 5.6, this one for a transportation vehicle. Although this might be a commercial venture, the WBS displayed is consistent with the DOD WBS standard in that level two breaks out: vehicle structure, testing, data, and an all-other category called project management.

The last two WBS illustrations are shown in Figures 5.7 and 5.8, which represent two types of software projects. Software projects are gaining in importance and would appear to represent a new frontier for project management. As of this writing, there appears to be no universal agreement as to what might constitute an acceptable software WBS format.

Make-or-Buy Choices ... A Critical Part of Scope Definition

One last point must be made about using a WBS to define a new project: The WBS must reflect the way that the project management team intends to manage the project, which should include the project manager's make-or-buy decisions. Make-or-buy choices come after the project has been adequately defined, but are an integral part of the complete project definition process.

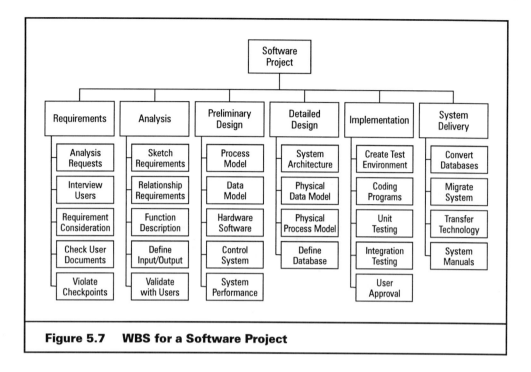

Figure 5.7   WBS for a Software Project

Stated another way, project scope definition is incomplete until the determination has been made as to what effort will be performed by one's own organization (company made), and what work will be procured (bought) from another company. It does make a difference. Procured project scope creates a legal relationship that, if not done correctly, can lead to energy-absorbing claims negotiations and the claims settlement process. The procurement of project scope is a subject of critical importance to the project manager. Make-or-buy choices should be reflected in the final WBS for a given project.

The WBS at level 2 often reflects the most critical part of the scope-definition process. Shown in Figure 5.9 is an illustration of a WBS for a construction project, but with three distinct management approaches displayed. All approaches need to be reviewed, because they illustrate the project manager's make-or-buy choice and hence the way that the project will be managed.

To the left side of Figure 5.9, in "-A-," is displayed one approach reflecting the project manager's make-or-buy choices. Under approach A, the design effort will be purchased from an external company. The common and/or high-value materials will be procured by the internal project team, perhaps to achieve a price advantage by the pooling requirements of multiple projects. Finally, the construction effort will be separately con-

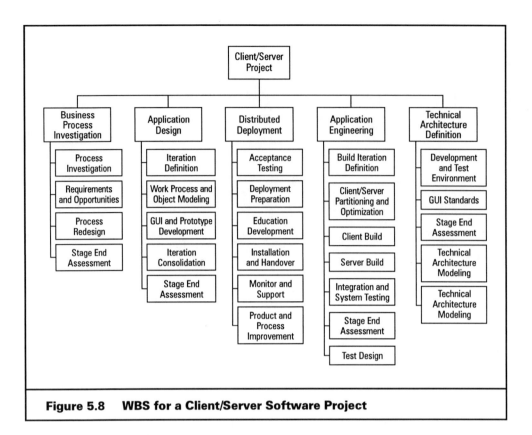

Figure 5.8   WBS for a Client/Server Software Project

tracted to another firm. This display is similar in approach to the WBS for the energy construction project shown in Figure 5.3. For purposes of simplicity, other important project work has not been displayed in the Figure 5.9 WBS—for example, final site checkout, project management, and so on.

Shown in the center ("-B-") of Figure 5.9 is a second approach in which the major project effort is divided into two major parts: the design effort and a construction effort, both of which will be procured. In this case, the construction contract will include the purchase of all materials.

The third approach is shown to the right ("-C-"), in Figure 5.9, in which case a single design-build contractor will be selected to perform the total design, procurement, and construction job on behalf of the owner.

The point of this discussion is that the WBS is a critical tool for the project manager's use to initially define the project and then describe how the project will be managed, also reflecting the make-or-buy determinations. All functions must have a say in the formation of the project WBS and, once approved, should conform to the format of the official WBS.

The WBS is vital in order to achieve an integrated project management approach and to measure project performance during the full life

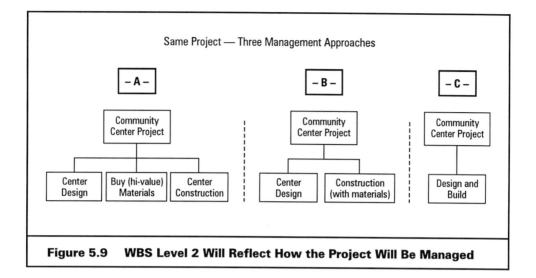

Figure 5.9   WBS Level 2 Will Reflect How the Project Will Be Managed

of the project. While all levels of the project WBS are important, level 2 in particular will describe the project management approach being implemented.

The WBS and Earned Value

From the beginning, the WBS has been an integral part of the earned value concept. A hierarchical structure (WBS) defining the project is required in order to integrate the various functions into a common project mission, and then to relate the requirements of the project to the company's permanent organizational units.

When the earned value concept was first introduced to industry as a part of the Cost/Schedule Control Systems Criteria in 1967, the DOD mandated thirty-five management-control system standards, or criteria, that must be met by any firm wishing to contract for a new major government acquisition. Interestingly, the very first of these thirty-five criteria addresses the issue of defining the project with the use of a WBS. This criterion read: "Define all authorized work and related resources to meet the requirements of the contract, using the framework of the contract work breakdown structure (WBS)" (DOD 1967).

In practice, under cost-reimbursable-type contracting, the owner of the project will typically define the first two or three levels of the WBS, representing the way that performance is to be monitored and reported during the life of the project. Typically, the project manager and the team then define the lower levels of the project, extending the WBS to represent the way that the work will be performed. Under fixed-price or lump-sum contracting, where the cost growth risks rest totally on the project manager, the project management team will define all levels of the WBS, representing how it intends to manage its project.

At the lowest level of each WBS element, the project will define a management-control point, which initially went by the term "cost account," but more recently is called a "control account." The control account is a critical point for performance measurement to take place, for this is where the integration of scope, schedule, and resources will take place and where the project will measure its performance throughout the duration of the project. The control account is the fundamental building block for EVPM and was defined some three decades ago as:

> COST ACCOUNT. A management control point at which actual costs may be accumulated and compared to the budgeted cost of work performed. A cost account is a natural control point for cost/schedule planning and control, since it represents the work assigned to one responsible organizational element on one contract work breakdown structure (CWBS) element (DOD 1967).

Initially the cost/control account was defined as the intersection point of a single WBS element with a single organizational unit. More recently, with the increasing popularity of integrated multifunctional project teams, the requirement for one organizational unit has been expanded to constitute one multifunctional team. Additionally, while the scheduling of activities may continue to take place deeply within detailed WBS elements, the use of multifunctional project teams has resulted in larger segments of defined work being done within control accounts at higher levels of the project WBS.

Thus, under the multifunctional project team approach, management will monitor the performance of less management control points—a more logical approach and one that has led to a reduction of some 90 percent in the total number of management points. A positive move.

Projects Should Use WBSs

One last issue needs to be addressed. There sometimes is an organizational conflict between the best interests of the projects and the best interests (the parochial objectives) of the functions who supply the resources to the projects. Because the functions will frequently support multiple projects at the same time, they may well have other priorities that compete or conflict with the requirements of any given project. Functions typically support multiple projects and employ a matrix form of organization. Individual functions often do not see the utility (to them) to operate within the confines of the project WBS, perhaps requiring that they lose their functional perspective.

For example, the cost-estimating function will typically have its historical cost data available in great detail, but likely collected and formatted along company functional-organizational lines. Unless specifically directed by senior management, it likely will not see the utility (to it) of reconstructing such data simply to match a given WBS for a single project.

Often the scheduling function will find a WBS environment too confining. Scheduling is a critical project function, and the people who perform this important role are unique individuals who will often best perform their creative work without restrictions of any sort. However, unless this critical function operates within the overall envelope of the project WBS, the opportunity for the project to integrate its work scope with the costs and schedules will be lost.

From an enterprise standpoint, only if all key project functions perform their work within the framework of the agreed-to project WBS—and, most particularly, the contracting, scheduling, estimating, and budgeting functions—will the project be in a position to adequately integrate its functional work and maximize project performance. Since many (perhaps most) organizations often consist of the sum of their individual projects, the successful performance of each project should be of major consequence to the firm, overshadowing the parochial goals of individual functions. The WBS, if properly defined at the outset, can constitute the vehicle to negotiate functional resources, set priorities, and measure performance in an integrated fashion throughout the full life cycle of a project.

One final point needs to be made. We have been attempting to make the case for the use of a WBS for two important purposes: 1) to define all project work down to detailed discrete tasks that can be individually managed, and 2) to integrate the various functional efforts into a common project framework. We can think of no better vehicle to accomplish this objective than the WBS. However, it would be misleading to suggest that the WBS must be used, or that it is the only vehicle to accomplish these goals. We know of projects that have been successfully performed that have employed the earned value concept and have not used a WBS. But they have substituted another vehicle for the WBS.

A company's organizational structure, if it is stable for the full project duration, may sometimes be used as a WBS substitute to integrate scope, schedule, and costs. The construction industry, which typically employs a simple form of earned value, but does not call it such, often uses construction historical standards, the Construction Specification Institute Codes, or other hierarchical standards as a method to integrate project tasks. Bottom line: The WBS seems to work best ... but other close substitutes may, on occasion, be used as a substitute for the WBS.

However, we recommend that all projects use the WBS to define and implement their work.

In Summary

We have been attempting to make a case for defining the project effort before starting to perform the work. Reaching an agreement between the owner and contractor, between the buyer and seller, on what constitutes the project scope is important to the success of any project. It is also critical to the employment of the earned value concept.

All this discussion reminds us of a statement made by a person who worked in project management. When asked if the projects at his site ever overran their costs, he immediately replied, "We never overrun our project costs ... any unfinished work gets moved into next year's projects."

Think about this remark for a minute. If one is given a budget to do a certain amount of work, then spends all of the money and ultimately moves all unfinished work into next year's projects, what do you call this condition? Answer: *an overrun!*

Scope management is vital to the effective management of any project. Understanding the scope of a project is perhaps of even greater importance when earned value is employed, because project performance must be measured throughout the life of the project ... from implementation until project closeout.

Scope management is perhaps a project manager's greatest challenge ... and it is also fundamental to the employment of the EVM concept. Unless the full scope is properly defined and then managed throughout the life of a project, the ability to meet the objectives of projects will be severely compromised.

Chapter 6

Plan and Schedule the Project

Understanding the Project

Previously we emphasized the importance of completely defining the full scope of any new project, and suggested that this effort is best accomplished using a generally accepted technique called the Work Breakdown Structure (WBS). We recommended that the full project management team precisely define what work it plans to perform ... including the outer limits of the project commitment. The WBS is a vehicle that allows for the progressive detailing of project tasks and the integration of such tasks with various organizational functions, in particular the contracting, estimating, budgeting, and scheduling functions, as well as those line functions that will be performing the defined work.

We refer to the WBS as a generally accepted technique because, while some industries have enthusiastically embraced the WBS as a project management tool, other industries have not. The construction industry, as an example, frequently relies on other methods to define its projects; perhaps most notable is the use of the Construction Specifications Institute's standard codes in lieu of using a WBS.

Of equal importance, by having a clear understanding of what scope of work the project has committed to do, it effectively defines what work has not been agreed to. Project managers must be cognizant of the full scope (and the limitations) of the projects that they set out to accomplish. They must be able to discern when the project has been completed, and know precisely when out-of-scope tasks are being requested. There is nothing wrong with doing out-of-scope work ... as long as one gets paid something extra for doing the added tasks. This is called "scope creep," and such creep must be tightly managed in order to avoid cost and schedule problems.

Now that we have an understanding of what we are going to do, it is time to take the next logical step in the process of implementing a new project that employs the earned value concept: we must plan and then schedule the project. The process of planning for any new project is no different than that used to employ earned value. A detailed bottoms-up plan is the preferred approach.

Planning the Project

Perhaps a good way to start a discussion on planning is to borrow a quote from Rudyard Kipling, a man who knew nothing about project management ... or did he? A century ago, this Englishman, who was born in India, gave us these profound words, which define nicely the process of project planning: "I keep six honest serving men (they taught me all I knew); their names are WHAT and WHY and WHEN and HOW and WHERE and WHO." Any project manager who could enlist the support of these six honest serving men would be well on the way to defining a viable project plan.

Just what is the project planning process? It all depends on whom you ask. One of the best descriptions of this process was given to us over two decades ago by a founding Project Management Institute (PMI) member, with the number of 007, a PMI Fellow, and a certified PMI Project Management Professional. We can think of no better description of project planning than that provided by this expert. He defined the project planning process as a ten-step iterative effort:

1. Define the project scope, and identify specific tasks with use of a WBS.
2. Assign responsibility for performance of each of these specific tasks.
3. Identify the interfaces between tasks.
4. Identify the key project milestones.
5. Prepare the master schedule.
6. Prepare the top budget.
7. Prepare detail task schedules.
8. Prepare detail task budgets.
9. Integrate the task schedules and budgets with the project master schedule and top budget.
10. Set up the project files (Archibald 1976).

Now what does all this mean? Well, to us it suggests first that project planning is an iterative process. It evolves. Planning becomes progressively more definitive with each cycle taken. Each iteration serves to reinforce the viability of the plan. The process works best when the full project team is involved, including, if possible, the project's owner or buying customer. Owner involvement not only produces good ideas, but also leads to customer buy-in or approval of the resulting plan. Any final project plan should identify specific individuals who will be held accountable for the performance of each of the defined project tasks.

We particularly like the focus on the last item, the setting up of project files. All too often this work is considered to be mundane and is often overlooked ... until the claims settlement process begins, and a team of people must then sift through a multitude of project documents in an attempt to make some order out of the chaos. Better to start these critical files early and maintain them throughout the full life cycle of the project.

The one additional step that we would like to add to the listing of project planning tasks is that of project "risk management." Risk identification, risk assessment, and risk mitigation are of vital importance to completing the project planning process and to the ultimate success of any project.

The risk management process will typically begin with an assessment of the potential risks as envisioned by the project team, which will focus on the known and anticipated risks for the project. The team will often use the framework of the WBS to lay out and conduct its initial risk assessment. After the project risks have been identified, they are then normally subjectively quantified as to the likelihood (probability) of the risk happening and to the impact (consequences) to the project, should the risk actually materialize.

A risk mitigation plan will begin to take form, often not necessarily eliminating such risks altogether, but by reducing them to acceptable levels. Risk mitigation planning will likely impact both the required allocation of project resources and require added (redundant) tasks to the project. Added resources, task redundancy, and what-if analysis will typically help to bring the project risks down to acceptable levels. Admittedly, we have described a rather simple form of risk management. Some projects will want to employ a more sophisticated approach for the management of their risks, using the various software tools available to them.

Additionally, it should be mentioned that the project managers of today have the finest array of software tools ever available to perform these critical tasks. These state-of-the art tools allow them to quickly plan their new projects, lay out the expected tasks, show the task interrelationships and constraints, expose potential risks, and model various "what-if" scenarios. There are numerous planning, scheduling, and critical path method (CPM) software packages available to the general public. The project CPM network serves to reinforce the viability of any new project plan, and, if reflected in a formal Project Master Schedule (PMS), it will provide assurances that the project will accomplish the project plan to the satisfaction of all vested parties.

Scheduling the Project

There is probably no single issue that has greater universal acceptance with project managers than on the need for and the benefits to be gained from formally scheduling every project. All projects need the schedule to formally implement their project plans. Larger projects may have multiple schedules requiring a formal scheduling system. But even the smaller projects need to have at least a single PMS in place.

The project schedule likely is the best tool available for managing day-to-day communications on any project. And, further, one of the best ways to control a project plan is to monitor performance regularly with use of a formal scheduling system.

In 1967, when the Department of Defense (DOD) initially released its thirty-five Cost/Schedule Control Systems Criteria (C/SCSC) implementing earned value, three of the criteria specifically dealt with the requirement to have a formal scheduling system. Earned value thus relies on the project schedule to provide a framework for allocating the authorized resources—that is, the authorized budgets.

All of the original 1967 earned value criteria were rewritten by industry in 1996, but the identical requirements for a formal scheduling system were maintained in three criteria, as follows:

> 6. Schedule the authorized work in a manner that describes the sequence of work and identifies the significant task interdependencies required to meet the requirements of the program.

> 7. Identify physical products, milestones, technical performance goals, or other indicators that will be used to measure progress.

> 23. Identify, at least monthly, the significant differences between both planned and actual schedule performance and planned and actual cost performance, and provide the reasons for the variances in the detail needed by program management (National Security Industrial Association 1996).

Question: Are these three criteria unique to earned value projects? Absolutely not. These three criteria lay down fundamental scheduling principles that would apply to any project anywhere in the world.

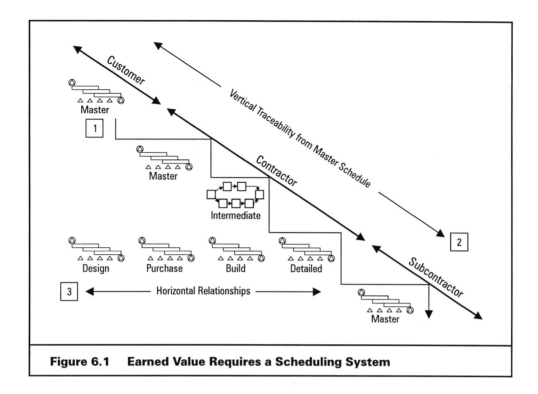

Figure 6.1   Earned Value Requires a Scheduling System

Since the DOD's earned value criteria were initially issued, certain interpretations have evolved as to what type of scheduling system may be required from projects in order to support the requirement. It is interesting to note that the demands for a formal scheduling process to support earned value can be reduced to three general requirements, as illustrated in Figure 6.1.

First, all earned value projects must have at least a single top-level summary schedule that defines the broad parameters of the project. This schedule would typically carry the title of "master schedule" or "Project Master Schedule" (PMS). Such schedules would be the exclusive property of the project manager and issued under the direction of that individual. The master schedule should be a controlled document, formally issued to all key functions and individuals working on the project.

On a small project, there may be only a single schedule needed, which would still carry the title of "master schedule." But as projects increase in size and complexity, the necessity of having one top schedule to specify the outer time parameters is of critical importance. All lower-tier intermediate and detailed project or functional schedules would, by definition, be subordinate to the project manager's master schedule. The requirement for a master schedule is displayed as item "1" in the upper left corner of Figure

6.1. Here the customer, the contractor, and the subcontractors have all issued their respective master schedules in concert with each other.

The second requirement for earned value projects is that the tasks or milestones described in all subordinate schedules must be in concert with the specific requirements contained in the PMS. All of the tasks and events depicted on lower-level project schedules must be relatable to the master schedule; that is, there must be what is called "Vertical Traceability" ("2" in Figure 6.1), going from the lower detailed schedules up to the requirements defined in the top schedule. It may be acceptable to be behind, relative to the requirements of the top schedule. However, it would be unacceptable to not know one's position as it relates to the PMS. The project manager's master schedule is supreme and must be followed on any project.

Vertical traceability simply means that all individuals working on a given project must know when the project manager requires their particular tasks to begin and end, consistent with the PMS. For example, on a construction-type job, all project schedules must support the same substantial completion date. On an aircraft development project, all schedules must support the same first flight date, and so forth.

When there are multiple organizational elements involved on any given project—as shown in Figure 6.1, where three separate entities are displayed ("Customer," "Contractor," "Subcontractor")—the issue of vertical traceability becomes critical. For example, the buying customer will specify its requirements in the form of a master schedule, which is typically incorporated as an exhibit into the prime contract. The prime contractor's master schedule must be issued in concert with the requirements of the customer's master schedule. Further, all subordinate subcontractor schedules likewise must be in concert with the requirements contained in the highest-level master schedule.

On projects of major size or complexity, where frequently multiple sites and companies are involved, project managers, out of necessity, have gone to a more formal controlled scheduling process. On such major projects, they will frequently employ some type of a scheduling hierarchy to pull together the various schedules. Shown in Figure 6.2 is a "scheduling tree," which is used to vertically link and integrate all project schedules. Each subordinate schedule represents a subproject to the master schedule and, ideally, major project milestones can be linked within each of the respective subordinate schedules.

Figure 6.2 reflects the hierarchy of the buying customer, the prime contractor, and the various subcontractors. It also displays the project's peculiar

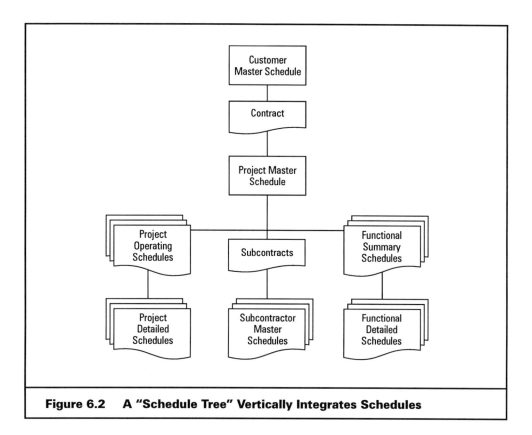

Figure 6.2   A "Schedule Tree" Vertically Integrates Schedules

schedules in the left column and the functional organizational schedules in the right column. The functional schedules for the various departments—for example, engineering—will also contain the tasks necessary to support each project. In the center are listed the various subcontractor schedules.

The third ("3" in Figure 6.1) and final requirement of scheduling in an earned value project environment is that there be "Horizontal Relationships" established between all dependent project tasks. Simply put, and as shown in the lower left-hand corner of Figure 6.1, the design must be available before materials can be purchased, and the materials must be available before the project deliverable can be built. Relationships and constraints between project tasks must be identified.

Interestingly, the creators of the original C/SCSC requirements and the more recent industry earned value management system rewrite have carefully avoided imposing any requirements for employing a specific scheduling methodology. Rather, they took the approach of merely specifying broad general requirements. Most particularly, they avoided requiring the use of the CPM. And yet, we know of no other way to isolate the horizontal task relationships and constraints, particularly on a complex project, than with use of CPM scheduling. Note that the two recent government initiatives of the 1990s, to be covered next, are very specific in their scheduling requirements. They both required CPM techniques.

Recent Government Initiatives Requiring CPM

Two governmental initiatives mandated in the early 1990s are worth noting because they both imposed rather specific schedule reporting requirements on the private sector. Both of these initiatives happened in the early 1990s, some twenty-five years after the C/SCSC were first issued, and both required the use of some type of critical path methodology on their projects.

When the United States (U.S.) Department of Energy (DOE) issued its project control system guidelines in 1992, it specifically required the use of CPM scheduling as a required technique to be employed on all its funded projects (U.S. DOE 1992). CPM networks were required to be an integral part of the management of all DOE projects.

Also of note, when the Canadian government released its new management control system guidelines in 1993 for private contractors to follow, it specified the use of CPM scheduling. The Canadian project guidelines were tailored after the U.S.' C/SCSC, but clearly required that earned value be used in conjunction with CPM network scheduling (Canadian General Standards Board 1993).

While the initial 1967 and revamped 1992 earned value criteria were silent on which scheduling methodologies were to be used, these two recent mandates for governmental project management specifically called out the use of CPM as a required scheduling technique.

Earned Value Requires a Scheduling System

In order to implement any form of earned value project management, two absolute rules have been discussed. First, you must define what it is you are about to do; that is, you must scope the entire project. The second requirement deals with the placement of the defined scope into a fixed time frame so that performance can be measured throughout the life of the project. Some might suggest that these two rules are not unique to earned value management, that they are fundamental to all good project management ... period. We would agree completely. Earned value simply requires that fundamental project management principles be employed.

Just how important is scheduling to earned value applications? We need to understand this issue in order to put earned value implementation on a proper footing.

In 1967, some four months prior to the formal release of the DOD's earned value C/SCSC, an industrial engineer with the U.S. Air Force, and one of the early architects of the modern-day earned value applications, described nicely the importance of scheduling in a paper that he wrote. He specified what was required in order to measure earned value, emphasizing the need for a controlled scheduling process. His message:

> As of a given point in time, we need answers to these questions:
> 1) What work is scheduled to have been completed?
> 2) What was the cost estimate for the work scheduled?
> 3) What work has been accomplished?
> 4) What was the cost estimate of the completed work?
> 5) What have our costs been?
> 6) What are the variances (Fitzgerald 1967)?

The central theme of his message can be summarized in just three words: scope, schedule, costs. Items 1 and 2 in his message cover the work scheduled and the costs for doing this work, which we call the planned value.

Items 3 and 4 cover the work performed and the costs for doing this work, which we call the earned value. We have not yet addressed his third issue, that of the cost estimate/budget, but we will in the next chapter. Note that the actual costs as described in item 5 have nothing to do with measuring either the planned value or the earned value, but must be related to the earned value.

However, it should be clear that in order to employ some form of earned value measurement, one must understand the work to be done and then manage that effort within a controlled time frame, that is, a scheduling environment.

There is one additional earned value criterion that should be mentioned, because it requires a formal scheduling process in order to *synchronize*, FIRST, the planned value of the work scheduled with the earned value of the work actually performed, and, SECOND, to relate the earned value against the actual costs for performing the work. This criterion reads as follows:

> 22. At least on a monthly basis, generate the following information at the control account and other levels as necessary for management control using actual cost data from, or reconcilable with, the accounting system:

71

1) Comparison of the amount of planned budget and the amount of budget earned for work accomplished. This comparison provides the schedule variance.

2) Comparison of the amount of the budget earned and the actual (applied where appropriate) direct costs for the same work. This comparison provides the CV (U.S. DOD 1996).

Item number 1 in this criterion requires the synchronization of the planned value with the earned value in order to isolate any planned Schedule Variance (SV). A negative earned value SV simply indicates to the project that it is falling behind its scheduled work.

Please note that the earned value SV may (sometimes) have no relationship to the project's critical path position, which is a more important matter for the project to monitor. Being behind in the work that the project set out to do will probably cost more to accomplish in a later time frame, but it may not extend the duration or completion date for the project. However, the critical path, if not managed aggressively, could extend the duration of the project and cost dearly in added resources to complete all of the required work. All earned value SVs and the project's critical path should be monitored together by the project manager.

Item number 2 of the criterion is the more serious of the two earned value variances. It is called the "Cost Variance" (CV), and it represents the relationship between the earned value accomplished versus the actual costs that it took to generate the earned value. A negative CV can result in permanent damage to the project's final cost requirements.

If a project spends more funds to perform the planned work than it has budgeted, then the resulting condition is plainly an overrun. Overruns, even early overruns, have been proven to be nonrecoverable by any project. Overruns are rarely (if ever) offset by subsequent performance, although many project managers have a tendency to be optimistic about their abilities to recover such losses. Historical experience would suggest that performance in later periods tends to get worse, not better, with the passage of time. The reason: the planning for later project periods tends to be progressively more vague, less well defined, and thus more subject to negative cost performance. The earned value CV is a critical indicator for any project manager to watch.

In Summary

In any project that employs earned value management, the project's time-phased performance plan (called the planned value) is a reflection of the work described in the PMS. The project's actual performance (its earned value) is derived by measurement of progress resulting from the same PMS. Stated in another way, without a project scheduling system, there could be no earned value performance measurement.

A scheduling system is fundamental to the successful management of all projects. And not coincidentally, basic scheduling is also a requisite to employing earned value project management.

Chapter 7

Estimate and Budget Project Resources to Form Control Account Plans (CAPs)

Once the technical requirements of the project have been properly defined, and all of the specified work planned and scheduled, the next logical step in establishing the project's baseline is to forecast how much each task likely will cost. The required resources must be estimated, quantified, and then specifically authorized by the project manager in the form of official project budgets. A cost estimate is only an estimate until the project manager approves it in the form of a budget.

These initial steps are required in order to employ the earned value concept on a new project. (Important Point: These steps are no different than the initial effort required to implement any new project. This is simply fundamental project management. But these steps are particularly critical to an earned value project, because once the baseline has been put into place, the actual performance against the baseline will need to be measured continuously for the duration of the project.)

However, there is one requirement that perhaps distinguishes earned value projects from most other projects. In order for performance measurement to take place during the term of the project, the project baseline needs to be created from detailed bottoms-up planning. Performance measurement with earned value projects takes place at the very bottom within management control cells, which carry the title of "Control Account Plans" typically referred to as CAPs. Within the CAP, the work to be done will be aligned with the authorized budget and within a definite time frame specified in the project master schedule.

Routinely (typically monthly, but sometimes weekly), the project manager will want to make an assessment of how well the project has been performing against the baseline. Project performance will be precisely measured employing earned value metrics, normally expressed as cost or schedule performance variances from the baseline. Such variances will give an "early warning" signal of impending problems and are used to determine whether or not corrective action needs be taken in order to stay within the commitments to management.

Figure 7.1. conceptually displays the process of taking these three initial steps to form an earned value project baseline (step four in Figure 7.1). The project baseline must be established, typically done in the sequence as shown in Figure 7.1. Step one is that the project's scope of work must be defined, often with use of a work breakdown structure (WBS), leading to a statement of work, which is then assigned to a functional organization for performance. Step two, the defined scope must be planned next and scheduled down to the detailed work package or task level. Finally, in step three, the required resources must be estimated and subsequently authorized in the form of official project budgets.

It must be mentioned that in some organizations, primarily those managing software projects, this conventional sequence is often altered. These organizations often will take step one to define their work, then perform step three to estimate the required resources, and finally take step two to schedule their work. They will change the typical project implementation sequence, because they may be severely constrained by the availability of qualified resources to work on their projects. There is nothing inherently wrong with this approach as long as organizations start with step one, the project definition process, and end up with an approved project baseline, as in step four, displayed in Figure 7.1.

The end objective of taking these three sequential steps—either as steps one, two, three, or alternately as steps one, three, two—will be the formation of step four, the detailed project baseline. The earned value project baseline is made up from the sum of the CAPs, which provide the measurable performance control points for the earned value projects. The significance of the control account needs to be clearly understood in order to properly utilize the earned value concept. But next we need to emphasize the importance of working with an "integrated" project baseline.

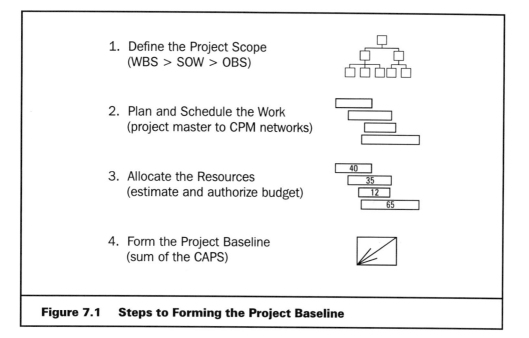

1. Define the Project Scope
   (WBS > SOW > OBS)

2. Plan and Schedule the Work
   (project master to CPM networks)

3. Allocate the Resources
   (estimate and authorize budget)

   40
   35
   12
   65

4. Form the Project Baseline
   (sum of the CAPS)

Figure 7.1   Steps to Forming the Project Baseline

Integrating the Project Scope of Work with Costs and Schedule

One somewhat unique aspect of employing the earned value concept is the fact that the technique requires that there be an integration of all vital components of the project. What does the term "integration" actually mean? Simply put, integration in earned value means that the technical scope of work, the work authorization, planning, scheduling, estimating, budgeting, cost accumulation, all of these processes must be aligned with the functions performing the actual work, and all integrated with use of the WBS. This concept was described in Figure 4.1 when we discussed the earned value body of knowledge. In Figure 4.1, the traditional nonintegrated approach was shown on the left side, while on the right side was illustrated an integrated earned value project approach.

Rarely is the full integration of these diverse activities ever achieved on a typical project. However, an integrated baseline is an absolute requirement with earned value management.

When the Cost/Schedule Control Systems Criteria (C/SCSC) were first issued in 1967, and later updated by industry in 1996, the requirement for the integration of these processes was clearly mandated in the third criterion:

3. Provide for the integration of the company's planning, scheduling, budgeting, work authorization, and cost accumulation processes with each other, and as appropriate, the program work breakdown structure and the program organizational structure (National Security Industrial Association 1996).

The integration of an earned value project is achieved with the creation of detailed CAPs, which are management control points placed at the desired levels of the project's WBS. The CAP is where the performance measurement takes place. Within each CAP, the planned tasks will be defined and then assigned to a specific functional organization for performance.

The cost and schedule and technical performance within each CAP can be summarized and then reported either to the top levels of the project WBS, for the benefit of the project manager, or related to various functional units, for the enlightenment of these managers.

Earned Value CAPs

At this time, we need to cover what is perhaps the single most important feature that distinguishes projects that employ earned value from projects that do not. This unique feature is the requirement to develop detailed, bottoms-up performance measurement baselines. The earned value performance baseline is made up from the individual CAPs. Originally termed Cost Account Plans (CAPs), industry in its 1996 update to the Department of Defense (DOD) C/SCSC substituted the term "control account plans" for "cost account plan," a positive move. The CAP is a management control point where the performance measurement must take place.

Additionally, and perhaps of greater importance, earned value is a technique for accurately relating the costs being spent against the physical work accomplished. This delicate relationship determines the cost performance efficiency factor being achieved on the project—what work was actually performed by the project for the costs that were actually spent. The cost efficiency factor is particularly critical because poor cost performance is nonrecoverable to the project. It has been empirically demonstrated for over three decades that whenever a project spends more money than the value of the physical work that it has accomplished, it does not subsequently correct this overrun condition. Historically, overruns only get worse, not better, with the passage of time.

Earned value requires that a detailed bottoms-up baseline plan be put in place. The baseline in earned value is formed with the creation of self-contained, measurable CAPs. The earned value technique can be employed on projects of any size, from as small as perhaps a few thousand dollars to mega-projects valued in billions of dollars. The concept is scalable, as long as certain fundamental principles are followed and the performance baseline is formed with use of measurable CAPs.

A little background on the term "control account plan" may be in order. In 1967, when DOD first issued its C/SCSC, it chose to call these measurement units by the term "cost accounts." A cost account was initially defined as the point of intersection of the lowest single WBS element with a single functional unit. More recently, with the general acceptance of the concurrent engineering (project teams) concept, the use of a single functional element has been broadened to include all functions working on a single WBS element. The subject of multifunctional teams will be addressed in the next section. Multifunctional project teams represent an important evolutionary development with earned value.

One important point on the use of CAPs: Four elements are required for earned value performance measurement (EVPM). Each CAP must include, at a minimum: 1) a discrete scope of work, typically expressed with work package tasks, 2) a time frame to complete each work package task, that is, the project schedule, and 3) the authorized project resources, the approved budget. Budgets may be expressed in any measurable form, for example, dollars, hours, units, and so on. Lastly, each CAP should have 4) a designated individual to manage the effort, typically called the Control Account Manager, or CAM. Most CAMs have a dual reporting relationship: to the project manager for the work and to the functional manager in their permanent organizations.

The CAP is the fundamental building block for performance measurement, and the summation of the CAPs will add up to the total project value. The project master schedule will set the planned time frame for each CAP, and then determine the EVPM using the same metrics that established the plan.

On smaller projects of only a few thousand dollars in value, there may be only a few CAPs required for the project. However, on larger projects of millions or even billions of dollars, there obviously will be more CAPs required out of necessity. In each case, the project manager must determine the appropriate number of CAPs to be used, their length, and their size.

There are no absolute standards to be recommended as to the appropriate size for CAPs. The determining rule of thumb should be whatever is manageable for a given scope of work. What is manageable will likely vary by the type of project being implemented. If the effort covers state-of-the-art research and development or routine product testing, continuous production, or a construction job, what will be considered manageable likely will be different in each case. Also, the amount of procured materials, the subcontracted work, the degree of personal supervision required, and the complexity of the effort will all play in the determination of what constitutes a manageable CAP.

The current trend in most earned value projects would appear to support the use of less in numbers, but larger-sized CAPs. It would also appear to support the use of multifunctional team CAPs, which will be covered next.

Multifunctional Team CAPs

The wisdom of earned value projects employing very small and very detailed CAPs, representing the intersection of a SINGLE WBS element with a SINGLE functional organization began to be questioned starting sometime in the mid-1980s. On larger multibillion-dollar mega-projects, the numbers of individual CAPs often ran into the thousands. This approach frankly was both cumbersome and impossible to manage. The amount of energy that it took to establish the initial planning and then to measure performance against hundreds or thousands of detailed CAPs required more effort than any perceived benefit to management.

Certain individuals working with earned value questioned the need for the use of small, short-span CAPs. Why not combine a larger segment of homogeneous work, perhaps representing a higher level of the WBS, and define it as a measurable CAP? As long as one maintained the relationship of work to budget, why not measure performance with larger groupings of work and a lesser number of CAPs?

The integrity of the CAPs had to be maintained. This meant that once a given scope of work was defined for a CAP, and the budgets authorized for the work, the delicate relationship of "defined work to authorized budget" had to be maintained until performance was completed. Indiscriminate transfers of either budget or work, independent of the other, between CAPs, would serve to distort performance measurement. Work once was defined and authorized with a budget; both must remain in concert. Preventing a shifting of work without corresponding funds, or vice versa, is an absolute rule in order to maintain the integrity of performance measurement within CAPs.

In addition to questioning the use of small CAPs, these same practitioners also questioned the necessity of measuring a single function within each CAP. Why not take a given segment of homogeneous work, and measure the collective results of all functions performing such work? Would not the performance of the full team be a more meaningful measurement than simply the performance of a single function?

Some initial resistance in the use of large multifunctional CAPs came from government review team directors; perhaps they were concerned that the necessary discipline was not present to prevent abuses. However, the DOD did later endorse the use of integrated work-team CAPs in its 1989 supplemental guidance statement:

> A natural fallout of the work team concept may be the overall reduction in the number of cost accounts with a resultant increase in their size, duration, and resource composition. This will result from grouping organizational elements, WBS elements, or a combination of both into larger, higher-level cost accounts (United States DOD 1989).

This policy change represented a major advancement in the use of the earned value within the DOD. If properly implemented at the beginning of a new project, the use of larger multifunctional work-team CAPs resulted in a reduction of 90 percent of total CAPs required for any project. Thus, with only 10 percent of the previous number of CAPs to monitor, management could now focus its attention on CAPs as viable management control points.

An interesting observation: Although the notion of employing larger, multifunctional, integrated cost accounts came from private industry, and was later approved for use by the DOD policy board, it was not implemented on new contracts to any significant degree. Rather, the entire approach was overtaken by other events of the same period. A new idea came along for the DOD project managers, which seemed to engulf the idea of larger multifunctional CAPs. The new direction was to be called "Integrated Product Teams" (IPTs).

A product development management concept called "concurrent engineering" had been in existence for years, and was starting to be noticed in both private industry and in certain quarters within the DOD acquisition community. The concurrent engineering initiative in fact overtook the need for multifunctional-team CAPs. Management gurus were also beginning to coin new terms to describe this exciting phenomenon, like "multi-functional projectization," whatever that term might mean (Peters 1992). It sounded a little like the old concurrent engineering concept, which was defined as:

> "Concurrent" or "simultaneous" engineering ... the means of carrying out the engineering process by forming a team whose members come from many disciplines. ... The normal activities of product design and development of manufacturing process are carried out in parallel rather than in a series, reducing the time it takes to perform both tasks (Slade 1993).

Some of the military program managers enthusiastically adopted the idea of the use of concurrent engineering, which they were to later call "Integrated Product Development Teams" (IPDTs). As with the initial earned value concept, the Air Force again took the lead and in 1990 issued the following policy statement urging the use of multifunctional integrated product development teams:

> Integrated Product Development (IPD) Teams: the integration of all functional disciplines required to manage the definition, development, acquisition, training, and support of systems for which we are responsible. The concept has been called "concurrent engineering," "integrated engineering," or "simultaneous engineering" in other organizations. Its principal feature is the merger of several functions in a single organization to ensure that all aspects of design, manufacturing, test, training, and support are addressed at all stages of the acquisition cycle, but particularly at the front end (Loh 1990).

Thus, the private industry initiative that urged the use of multifunctional work-team CAPs for earned value applications was quietly made a part of the larger DOD procurement initiative promoting the use of IPDTs. Earned value benefited from the use of multifunctional CAPs, allowing management to focus on a more meaningful but lesser number of control points. Conversely, the DOD project directors have better accepted and have adopted the earned value concept as their own valuable management tool, as a part of their initiative on using IPDTs. It was a win-win result for all parties in the management process.

We recommend the employment of earned value project management with use of multifunctional team CAPs for use on all projects within the private sector. The integrated project team, to us, represents a natural subdivision of the project into subprojects that align nicely with the project WBS.

Shown in Figure 7.2 is the use of earned value multifunctional team CAPs. Each CAP requires four elements to be viable: scope of work, schedule, budget, and team leader to manage the effort.

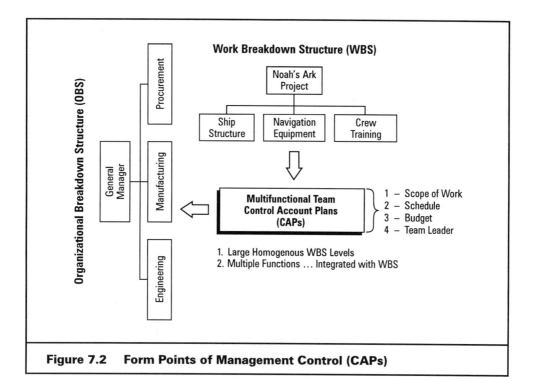

Figure 7.2   Form Points of Management Control (CAPs)

Estimates versus Budgets ... and Management Reserves

An opinion: All project managers need some type of "just-in-case" reserves to carry out their challenging work. Such funds are sometimes called "contingency budgets," other times, "management reserves." These values are simply set-aside amounts over and above the allocated budget values that await the misfortunes that too often come to projects ... they always have, and they likely always will. In scheduling, such management reserves will take the form of slack or float, which are time reserves, in addition to the cost reserves.

One important issue facing any project manager: Who should control these monetary or time reserves? Our position: Assuming such values can be uncovered, and this is not always an easy task, the project manager should own and control such contingency funds and schedule float. Why? For this answer, we go to an established authority on the subject of project management, who commented on the issue several years back:

> It is a natural tendency on the part of every person to provide a certain amount of cushion or reserve in his or her time and cost estimates. ... If approved, then each person will tend to expend all the time and cost available ... as Parkinson has said: "The work at hand expands to fill the time available. Expenditures will rise to meet the budget" (Archibald 1992).

If a project manager allows more time in the schedule than is needed to perform the tasks, then somehow people have a tendency to take all the time that has been authorized, and the excess time likely will cost more money. Also, if more funds are approved than are needed to accomplish the defined work, somehow these funds typically will get spent.

We would like to make a distinction between an estimate and an authorized budget. Authorizations will typically take the form of an approved budget or an approved schedule. An estimate may well represent the amounts that the person feels will be necessary to accomplish a particular task. However, as we all know, estimates sometimes (perhaps quite often) contain the estimated value needed to perform a task, PLUS a just-in-case amount to cover contingencies, or expected losses in negotiations, or possibly both.

Only the very young and inexperienced would seem to provide true, honest estimates. Stated another way, there would seem to be a high correlation between gray hairs and estimates that include contingency pads! Project contingencies may be needed, but they must be owned and controlled by the project manager, or else they may well be needlessly consumed.

What most of the more astute project managers have learned to do is authorize only what is needed to actually accomplish the work. Any differences are kept by the project manager for the potential problems that likely will happen, but just cannot be predicted in advance.

In Summary

In a project that employs the earned value management concept, the project's measurable performance plans will be formed with the creation of CAPs, placed at appropriate levels within the project's WBS. The WBS serves as an integrator of all activities for the project, and allows the defined work in the CAPs to be assigned directly to the functional organizations performing the work.

The formation of CAPs is the last of four implementation planning steps necessary to form an earned value baseline: 1) define the scope, 2) plan and schedule the work, 3) add the necessary resources to form CAPs, and 4) form the project baseline against which performance will be measured through to the completion of the total project.

What we have been describing is simply fundamental project management principles that should be applied to all projects.

Chapter 8

Establish the Earned Value Project Baseline

Introduction

Some project managers refer to it as their "stake in the ground." Others describe it simply as a "point of reference." Whatever it may be called, all projects need to establish some type of baseline against which performance may be measured during the project's life cycle.

This requirement is true for any project. But it is particularly critical for any project that employs earned value. Once under way, projects utilizing earned value will need to know precisely how much work they have physically accomplished—for example 15, 16, or 17 percent, in order to be able to predict with some degree of confidence how long it will take to finish the project, and how much the total bill might run.

A project baseline is needed in order to determine precisely how much of the planned work has been accomplished as of any point in time. The completed (earned) work is compared against the work that projects originally set out to do to assess their planned schedule status. The completed (earned) work is also compared against the actual consumed resources to reflect their cost true position.

Returning again to the experience gained from the Department of Defense when it first issued the cost/schedule control systems criteria in 1967, and later when these same criteria were reissued by industry in 1996, the requirement to establish a project measurement baseline has been consistent:

8. Establish and maintain a time-phased budget baseline, at the control account level, against which program performance can be measured. Initial budgets established for performance measurement will be based on either internal management goals or the external customer negotiated target cost including estimates for authorized but undefinitized work. Budget for far-term efforts may be held in higher level accounts until an appropriate time for allocation at the control account level. ... (National Security Industrial Association 1996).

The project manager must maintain the authorized baseline and approve or reject all changes to the baseline. Each change must be incorporated into the approved baseline.

The term "Control Account Plan" (CAP), a management control point, is the core for earned value measurement. CAPs are placed at selected elements of the Work Breakdown Structure (WBS), as determined by the project manager.

Each CAP must contain three discrete elements in order to be viable: 1) a specific scope of work, 2) a time frame for performance, and 3) an approved budget to accomplish the work. Each CAP must have the capability of measuring its planned value against the earned value, and also the earned value against the actual costs. A project's total Performance Measurement Baseline (PMB) is therefore merely the summation of its individual CAPs.

We will need to understand the makeup of the project baseline. Particularly, we should understand how earned value is initially planned and then measured within each of the CAPs and the methods used to accomplish this.

Methods Used to Plan and Measure Earned Value

The earned value concept depends upon the project scheduling system to provide the platform for performance measurement. Without a scheduling system in place, performance measurement could not take place. A project scheduling system will, by definition, reflect the project's scope of work, and then place all the defined work into a specific time frame for execution. When one adds resources to the scheduling system, and the metrics to plan and consume such resources, the earned value performance plan is in place.

The determination as to which metrics should be used to measure a particular application is a personal, judgmental issue and will vary by project. We will review the various options available to a project. But the project

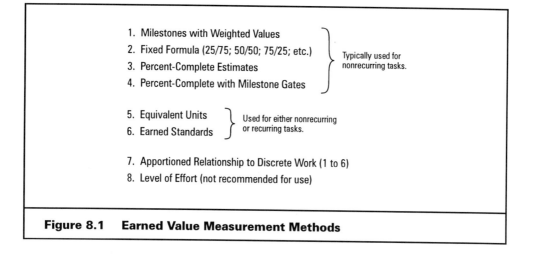

1. Milestones with Weighted Values
2. Fixed Formula (25/75; 50/50; 75/25; etc.)
3. Percent-Complete Estimates
4. Percent-Complete with Milestone Gates
} Typically used for nonrecurring tasks.

5. Equivalent Units
6. Earned Standards
} Used for either nonrecurring or recurring tasks.

7. Apportioned Relationship to Discrete Work (1 to 6)
8. Level of Effort (not recommended for use)

Figure 8.1   Earned Value Measurement Methods

team and the various work-package and control-account managers must ultimately select those measurement metrics that best support their particular needs. Ease of measurement and consistent applications are the keys.

Over the years, since earned value was introduced to industry, a number of methods have been employed to measure performance. For purposes of summarization, we have grouped these various methods into eight broad generic categories, as listed in Figure 8.1. We will discuss each of these measurement methods to provide an understanding of each.

The initial six of the eight methods listed deal with discrete types of performance measurement, which is always the preferred type to use.

1. **Weighted milestones**: This method of measurement works well and is typically used whenever individual work packages exceed a short span in duration, perhaps running two or more performance periods (weeks or months). The long work packages are converted into objective milestones to reflect finite divisions of work, preferably one or more in each period being measured. Each milestone is assigned a specific budgeted value, which will be earned upon physical completion of the event. The total work-package budget is divided, based on a weighted value assigned to each milestone.

The weighted-milestone method is a preferred method used in performance measurement, but it is also the most difficult to initially plan and then to administer. This method requires a close working relationship between the work-package managers, the scheduling people, and the resource-estimating people in order to set meaningful milestones for all work.

2. **Fixed formula by task: 25/75, 50/50, 75/25, and so on**: This approach was most popular in the early years of earned value, but its use has

diminished in more recent years. Conceptually it is perhaps the easiest to understand, but it requires very detailed and short-span work packages to make it work successfully.

We have specified only three values for this type of measurement, but, in fact, any distribution that adds to 100 percent may be used (10/90, 20/80, 60/40, and so on). We have also dropped the 0 to 100 percent approach because this is simply weighted milestones, covered earlier.

For example, the 25/75 method works well applied to those work packages that are scheduled to start and be completed within one or two measurement periods. A 25 percent value is earned when the activity starts, and 75 percent of the budget is earned when the task is completed. Purchased materials often work well with this method; 25 percent is earned when the materials are ordered, and the final 75 percent is earned when the materials arrive and are consumed.

3. **Percent-complete estimates**: This method allows for a periodic (weekly or monthly) estimate of the percentage of work completed to be made by the individual in charge of a given work package. Generally, for ease of administration, such estimates are expressed as a cumulative value against the full (100 percent) value of the work package.

Typically such estimates are made purely on a "subjective" basis, that is, one's personal and professional but yet unsubstantiated estimate. Thus, if people want to play games with earned value by claiming more value than they actually have, the subjective percent-complete estimate is where it will happen.

Over the years, the percent-complete method of estimating performance has received increasingly wide acceptance with industry. The reason: it is the easiest to administer of all earned value methods. But it is also the method most subject to performance pressures from senior management and individual bias.

There is nothing inherently wrong with the use of subjective estimates of results, as long as the work packages are well defined and senior internal management goes through periodic reviews of status to assess the reasonableness of subjective estimates. Many a heated debate has taken place between work-package managers and supervisors (sometimes also from their colleagues) when it is felt that individuals were claiming too much value for their respective work packages. Rarely are disagreements centered on too little value claimed, except perhaps at year-end bonus time!

If a company is genuinely utilizing the earned value method in the performance of a project, then the individual professional integrity of both employees and supervisors will often provide a sort of informal "check and balance" on the accuracy of the periodic estimates. Conversely, if a firm is giving lip service only to earned value, periodic subjective estimates can have wide distortions in measuring earned value.

Some firms have established internal written procedural guidelines (checks) on specific categories of costs to more accurately assign percent-complete values, based on actual work accomplishment. By providing such guidelines to work-package managers, some degree of objectivity is added to the subjective estimates. Examples of these guidelines may be: planning completed, lines of code released, drawings issued, materials ordered, parts received, tool orders released, and so on.

Another good practice that is sometimes used to buffer optimism when using the percent-completion method is to set a maximum ceiling allowed for any work package until it is 100 percent complete. While these percentages do vary from company to company, an 80 to 90 percent ceiling is a typical value for many firms. Thus, with an 80 percent ceiling in place, a given work package may earn only up to 80 percent of the manager's sub-jective estimate until the task is 100 percent complete, at which time the balance will be earned.

4. **A combination of percent-complete estimates with milestones used as gates**: Private industry has typically embraced the use of percent-complete estimates to set earned value measurements, probably because they are easiest to use. The manager of a work package merely assesses the status of the work package, perhaps compares its progress with some personal metric, written or not, and estimates the cumulative value accomplished.

Whatever progress value is selected, the work-package manager knows that he or she must defend the estimated value before fellow associates and before more senior management. Personal gaming with the estimates, unduly optimistic assessments, will ultimately come back to haunt the individual work-package manager.

If the project manager and company management have genuinely endorsed the earned value concept, then the subjective estimates by individual work-package managers have proven to be quite accurate. In fact, when work-package managers' personal reputations are at stake—when they know that management will hold them accountable for accurate earned value assessments—these managers tend to be on the conservative side, and will often slightly understate performance values to give themselves a cushion for next month's status report.

However, over the years, many of the government's earned value review teams seem to have great suspicion, little confidence, in the accuracy of purely subjective work-package estimates. Perhaps they have valid reasons. Subjective estimates of earned value performance do work well, but ONLY if there is a check and balance in place to challenge the false or overly optimistic estimates. It all depends on the degree to which the project managers and more senior managers have accepted earned value as a management tool. If company management employs earned value simply because it is a government mandate, then the validity of subjective estimates well may be questionable.

As a general rule, government review teams like the use of objective or tangible milestones for performance measurement. But the difficulty with weighted milestones is that they require considerable time and energy to put into place. Some feel that an inordinate amount of energy is required to plan a full baseline made up of weighted milestones.

Recently, there has been an evolution in earned value applications that seems to have captured the best of both measurement techniques: the ease of subjective percent-complete estimates used in conjunction with hard, tangible milestones. Such milestones are placed intermittently as "performance gates." Subjective estimates of performance are allowed up to a certain preset value for each milestone. However, these subjective estimates cannot go beyond a given milestone until certain predefined and tangible criteria have been met.

This method seems to work well in any industry and on any type of project. Thus, the broad universal acceptance of earned value may well be the result of finding the right balance between ease of implementation coupled with accurate performance measurement. Subjective estimates with milestones as gates may provide that balance.

Three specific examples will be discussed as we cover the use of CAPs in the private sector.

5. **Equivalent completed units**: This method allows for a given planned value to be earned for each full unit of work completed, or sometimes for a fractional equivalent of a full unit. The equivalent-completed unit approach works well when the project periods are of an extended duration, and it is also used for the management of repetitive-type work.

Assume that a project represents the construction of ten homes valued at $100,000 per home. The construction cost engineers will have prepared a detailed bottoms-up estimate for each of the planned homes, subdividing each home into individual cost elements. For example, the costs covering the site excavation for each unit may be estimated to be 10 percent of the total value for each house, perhaps set at $10,000 per house unit.

At the end of the first month, the project manager may want to quantify the earned value for the full project. The first month's effort may have consisted of the completion of the excavation of sites for all ten homes. Thus, the earned value for the first month would be calculated at $10,000 (for each completed excavation) times ten homes, or $100,000 in total. The measured earned value for the full project will be the equivalent of one full home ($100,000), although not one home will have been completed.

The construction industry uses this approach in making progress payments to their suppliers, using a simple but effective form of earned value. However, in construction, this method of calculating performance is often referred to as a "schedule of values," and rarely is the term "earned value" used. But conceptually it is the earned value method: relating actual physical progress against actual costs.

6. **Earned standards**: The use of planned standards to initially budget and then to subsequently measure the earned performance of repetitive-type work is perhaps the most sophisticated of all the methods, and requires the most discipline on the part of the participants. It requires the prior establishment of equivalent unit standards for the performance of the tasks to be worked. Historical cost data, time and motion studies, and so on are all essential to the process of measuring performance against work standards.

This type of work measurement is often done by the industrial engineers who originated the earned value concept in the first place. Interestingly, the industrial engineers typically refer to this method as equivalent work measurement rather than earned value. But it is the identical concept.

There is no single method of setting earned value that works best for all types of activity. Probably the best approach for any firm to take is to allow for multiple measurement methods to be used, and the one employed for individual work packages will be based on the collective judgments of the CAP managers working closely with industrial engineers. The use of earned standards is typically limited to repetitive or production-type work.

7. **Apportioned relationships to other discrete work packages (items 1 through 6)**: An apportioned task is the work that has a direct intrinsic performance relationship to another discrete work package, called a "measurement base" task. Measurement bases for apportioned tasks could be represented by any of the six previously described discrete methods.

One such example of an apportioned relationship might be that of "factory inspection," which typically would have a direct performance relationship to the "factory fabrication" labor that it would be inspecting.

However, the inspection budgets likely would be set at a different value (perhaps only 5 percent) of the factory-fabrication labor base. When the (apportioned) labor for factory inspection would be planned, it would be set with a direct alignment to its base work package, the factory fabrication labor. Later, when the earned value for factory fabrication labor might be set at a cumulative 48 percent, the factory inspection work would accept an identical performance value of a cumulative 48 percent.

When measuring the earned value "schedule" position for apportioned tasks, the values used will always reflect the same percentage (earned value) as that of its related discrete base. Since the time phasing of the planned value for the inspection will always match that of the fabrication labor, any SVs reflected by the fabrication labor, positive or negative, would be similarly reflected with the apportioned factory inspection work.

However, "cost" relationships for apportioned tasks can be substantially different from their base tasks. A Cost Variance (CV) for the apportioned work package will reflect the difference between the earned value achieved for the base work package versus the actual costs incurred for the apportioned work. The CV position of the (apportioned) inspection effort may be substantially different from that of the fabrication labor, because the inspection work package will relate the same earned value percentage versus whatever actual costs the inspection work may have incurred. Thus, if the manager of the inspection work package were to double the number of inspectors from those set in his or her budget, the inspection (apportioned) work package could reflect a negative CV, even though the base effort for fabrication labor might be reflecting a different CV position.

An apportioned work package will always reflect an identical schedule position from that of its base work package, because the planned value and earned value will be the same for both tasks. However, CVs may be substantially different for the apportioned work package, because CVs will reflect the apportioned actual costs, which may be higher or lower than their budgeted amounts.

8. **Level of Effort (LOE) ... not recommended for use**: LOE activities are those that may be necessary to support a project, but that are more *time* driven than *performance* related. Examples of such activities might be the project manager and immediate staff, scheduling, budgeting, procurement, contract administration, field engineering, security guards, cooks, bottle washers, help desks, and so on.

Whenever these functions are charged directly to a contract, they normally start at the beginning of the effort and continue for the full term of a project. However, they will generally have no measurable or deliverable outputs. One could make the case that these tasks should be better charged into an overhead pool, but that is a different issue.

The problem with LOE work packages is that whatever is authorized in the plan, the planned value automatically becomes the earned value for the project ... regardless of what physical work takes place. LOE tasks automatically earn whatever is approved in their plan, up to the limits of the planned value. Earned value always matches the planned value, regardless of whether any physical work was done or not! Dumb!

For example, if the planned value were approved for ten field engineers, but only two engineers actually worked, then the earned value would show as ten—precisely what was in the plan. There would be a zero Schedule Variance (SV), because earned value always matches the planned value with LOE work packages.

However, since the performance measurement was set at ten, but actual costs incurred were for only two, the CV for the period would be a positive 500 percent CV! Stated another way, the cost performance efficiency factor for field engineering in this period would be a plus five times perfect performance. These may seem like absurd examples, but with LOE tasks, the absurd will happen. Is this performance measurement? We think not. LOE work packages tend to distort the discrete measurement in the project and often mask bad performance. The only issue is how much distortion is acceptable.

Perhaps a real-life story may help. On a given project to develop a new high-technology vehicle, engineering was behind schedule in the release of its design. It was clearly behind in its schedule performance; that is, the earned value performance was not keeping up with the planned schedule. Strangely, the factory tooling was right on schedule and was actually underrunning its costs. How could this miracle happen: engineering was behind in its design, but manufacturing was making tools? Incredible.

A quick review indicated that the engineering tasks were being measured discretely, as was appropriate. However, tooling had unilaterally changed the earned value measurement methodology from discrete to LOE. It was showing earned value performed although the delivery of tools was running seriously behind schedule. Fortunately, the project scheduling system independently indicated a disconnect between the positive LOE earned value performance and the deficient completion of actual tools.

We recommend that zero LOE be used on projects. If a given work package cannot be planned as discrete work, or alternatively cannot be apportioned to other discrete tasks, then perhaps it should be considered as a candidate for indirect work, or perhaps eliminated altogether. LOE is not performance measurement. LOE is only the measurement of time.

Control Account Plans (CAPs)

Within earned value projects, the point at which performance will be monitored and measured is a generic type of management control cell referred to as a Control Account Plan, or simply a CAP. Prior to the rewrite of the earned value criteria by industry in 1996, the same term CAP was used, but at the time it stood for cost account plan. Both terms were identical in concept, although the title "control account plan" is likely more representative of the intended purpose of these cells.

The project manager will place CAPs at selected points within the project's WBS. This concept was discussed earlier and illustrated with Figure 4.1, with the earned value CAP shown on the right side of the display. CAPs may be placed at selected levels in a WBS—at levels 2, 3, 4, down to the lowest point where management will want to control a homogenous grouping of work.

The CAP is what management will manage during the performance of an earned value project. It is that point where the project's authorized work, resources, and time requirements will all be integrated. Within the CAPs, the cost and schedule performance indices will emerge, telling management where it must take action. The CAP in earned value is the fundamental building block that forms the project's measurement baseline.

Each CAP will be a self-contained management control cell. In order to be viable, each CAP must contain certain elements. Examples of these eight elements are listed in Figure 8.2.

Items 1, 2, and 3, as listed in Figure 8.2, represent the integration of scope with schedule and costs. Earned value requires an integrated baseline. Item 4 requires a designation of someone to be held responsible for the performance of each CAP, typically carrying the title of control account manager. While there are no absolute rules for what is to be contained in the CAPs, the eight elements listed in Figure 8.2 are fairly typical. At a minimum, each CAP must define the scope, schedule, costs, and also the responsible person, as indicated by items 1 through 4 in Figure 8.2.

Budgets for CAPs may take any measurable form: dollars, hours, units, standards, and so on—any value that can be quantified and subsequently measured. Indirect costs may or may not be included within the various

---

Control Account Plan (CAP)

1. Statement of Work (brief scope description)
2. Schedule (start/stop dates for each task)
3. Budget (expressed in dollars, hours, or units)
4. Responsible Person (control account manager)
5. Responsible Department (vice president)
6. Type of Effort (nonrecurring or recurring)
7. Division into Discrete Work Packages
8. Method Used to Measure EV Performance (milestone, formula, percent-complete, standards, apportioned)

Figure 8.2   Elements of a CAP

CAP budgets. Some firms hold their project managers responsible for total costs, including indirect costs, while others hold the project manager accountable for only direct costs, or possibly only direct hours.

Indirect costs may or may not be included within each CAP. Sometimes indirect costs are simply added to the top project value, perhaps conveniently housed in a separate CAP containing only indirect costs. The only absolute rule for budgeting is that all project dollars must be accounted for by the project, and that whatever was budgeted to a project to form the planned value must also be measured to reflect the earned value. Some organizations hold their project managers responsible for direct costs only, or direct hours only, and have a finance person convert the budgeted project metrics into the top budget dollar values. The responsibility for project costs will vary from company to company. More on this later.

Displayed in Figure 8.3 is a sample CAP, which lists four discrete work packages. Each of the four work packages shown has a separate line available to display the planned value, earned value, and actual costs for each work package. This is a simple six-month CAP, but may serve to illustrate important points. The four discrete work packages, as shown, use four different earned value approaches to plan and measure their performance.

Work Package #1 uses the weighted milestones method. Five milestones are listed in Figure 8.3. Each milestone carries a discrete value for the milestone, with the total budget set at 300. The milestone shown in January must be completed in total before the value of fifty can be earned. Discrete milestones are like an "on/off" switch: each milestone must be 100 percent complete before the value of the milestone can be claimed.

Control Account Plan (CAP)									
Work Packages	EV Method	Item	Jan	Feb	Mar	Apr	May	Jun	BAC
Work Package #1	Weighted Milestones	Plan	△50	△75	△75	△50	△50		300
		Earn							
		Actual							
Work Package #2	Fixed Formula (25/75)	Plan	△25	△75	△25	△75	△25	△75	300
		Earn							
		Actual							
Work Package #3	Percent-Complete Estimates	Plan	[100	100	100	100	100	100]	600
		Earn							
		Actual							
Work Package #4	Percent-Complete with M/S Gates	Plan	[100	100 33%△	100	100 67%△	100	100] 100%△	600
		Earn							
		Actual							
Total CAP	n/a	Plan	275	350	300	325	275	275	1800
		Earn							
		Actual							

Figure 8.3   A Sample CAP

Work Package #2 in Figure 8.3 has three tasks, each with a value of 100, the sum of which has a budget at completion of 300. This work package uses the fixed formula of 25/75 to plan and measure the performance of each of the one month-long tasks. When a given task is opened, the earned value is set at twenty-five, and only on completion of this task can the other seventy-five be claimed. The fixed formula method works well for short-term tasks.

Work Package #3 employs a manager's percentage-complete estimate to measure earned value performance. This method is the most simple to calculate, but it is also the technique that is most potentially subject to "gaming" by a work-package manager. Percentage-complete estimates work well because they are easy to administer, but they also must be watched closely by supervisors, who provide the "checks" on overly optimistic claims for earned value performance. Pressures to perform can result in overly optimistic calculations of earned value, which will temporarily distort the performance measurement.

Work Package #4 uses the combination of (subjective) percent-complete estimates combined with (objective) milestone gates to keep the estimates honest. Here the responsible work-package manager may subjectively estimate the value of work earned up to 200, at which point certain predefined performance criteria must be met before the 200 value can be exceeded. The percent-complete estimate with milestone gates incorporates the best of both techniques: each of administration, combined with accurate measurement.

One important point needs to be stressed on the relationship of the planned value (budget) to the earned value. The planned value (budget) effectively sets the "ceiling" for the earned value that may be claimed for each work package. For example, Work Package #1 in Figure 8.3 sets the total planned value budget (called the "Budget at Completion," or BAC) at 300 for the completion of all five milestones. The value of 300 is all that can be claimed for the completion of these five milestones. Should the completion of these five milestones require the expenditure of 500, or even 1,000, in order to finish, all that can be earned is the total of the planned value of 300, nothing more.

CAPs in the Private Sector

There are some very positive trends occurring within private industry in the use of earned value to manage its projects. These trends are the result of private industry innovating, experimenting, with the technique and using the concept in ways that make sense to its key customers: themselves as project managers. Many project managers have found an exciting new tool to help them manage their endeavors.

As we continue to attend various international conferences—for example, the annual Project Management Institute's Seminars & Symposium—we find more and more professional papers being delivered on earned value projects. Interestingly, many of these papers are describing earned value applications in ways never previously possible in the more formal, government-mandated applications. Industry has taken hold of earned value.

One of the more interesting trends is in the size of the CAP, the point where earned value is initially planned and subsequently measured. The size of earned value CAPs has been on the increase, and this alone will make the concept more useful as a project management tool. The increased size of the control point is the result of two changes in the definition of what constitutes an earned value CAP.

In the first place, project managers are focusing their attention on larger segments of homogenous work. They are focusing on higher levels of the WBS, and thus incorporating greater segments of project scope within each CAP. Additionally, they are including all functions performing this work. Thus, with the use of larger CAPs set at higher levels of the WBS, and the inclusion of all functions supporting the CAP, project management focuses its attention on less, but more critical, control points for its projects.

In addition, both industry and government are starting to employ a combination of measurement methods to plan and then measure earned value performance. The use of a combination of (subjective) percent-complete estimates, in conjunction with discrete (hard) milestones as measurement gates, provides ease of use with objective measurement.

Three examples of earned value applications are worth reviewing because they may well represent the future trend, as the concept expands from a government-imposed requirement into the private sector, because the project managers have found utility with the technique.

Case # 1: CAPs Used on a Development Project for a High-Technology Vehicle

Shown in Figure 8.4 is an example of a large multifunctional CAP to develop a high-technology project, spanning several years in performance. This CAP employed a combination of methods to measure earned value performance. For the first two phases, it employed the CAP manager's (subjective) percent-complete estimate used in conjunction with tangible (hard) milestones with advancement criteria as gates. In the later phase, it used fixed formula tasks (25 percent to start and 75 percent when completed) for the final effort. It worked! Performance was accurately measured over a multiyear period.

The detailed initial planning was the key. It took the cooperation of various functions. First, the technical management had to accept earned value as a management tool. The project manager and the chief engineer gave the concept their full endorsement, and the other technical managers, including the multifunctional team leaders, followed senior management's example. This major or super CAP, as illustrated in Figure 8.4, was effectively an amalgamation of several subordinate CAPs, each defined within the framework of the project WBS. The estimating, budgeting, and scheduling functions met with the various technical team leaders to establish their performance plans.

The CAP was separated into three distinct parts, which collectively constituted 100 percent of its total effort. Part one represented the conceptual layout work and was estimated to be 30 percent of the total design effort. Part two was designated "Assembly Layouts" and represented

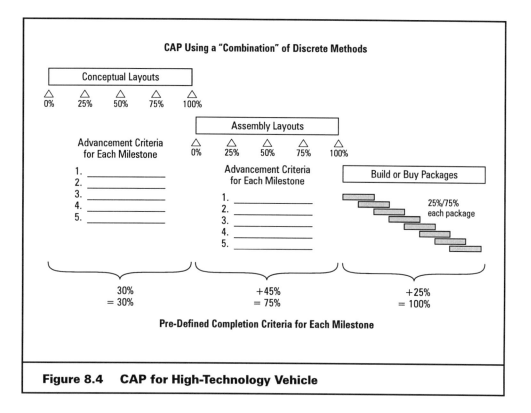

CAP Using a "Combination" of Discrete Methods

Conceptual Layouts

0% 25% 50% 75% 100%

Advancement Criteria
for Each Milestone

1. _____
2. _____
3. _____
4. _____
5. _____

Assembly Layouts

0% 25% 50% 75% 100%

Advancement Criteria
for Each Milestone

1. _____
2. _____
3. _____
4. _____
5. _____

Build or Buy Packages

25%/75%
each package

30%
= 30%

+45%
= 75%

+25%
= 100%

Pre-Defined Completion Criteria for Each Milestone

Figure 8.4   CAP for High-Technology Vehicle

another 45 percent of the total job. The final phase consisted of a series of small manufacturing build and procurement-buy packages and represented the final 25 percent of the job.

Parts one and two used the same earned value approach. They would both use the CAP manager's estimated percent-complete value to set the cumulative position each month. However, because each phase constituted a large dollar-value segment of work, the conceptual phase alone represented 30 percent of the total job; phases one and two would be subdivided into four performance segments, each represented by a specific completion milestone. Milestones would be set for the four subphases, representing the 25 percent, 50 percent, 75 percent, and 100 percent point of completion for the work.

These four milestones would act as "gates." The CAP manager would (subjectively) estimate the earned value position to be anywhere from 0 to 25 percent for the initial work in the conceptual phase. However, to get past the 25 percent milestone gate, the CAP had to meet certain predefined (specific) advancement criteria, which were previously established and approved by management. Once these selected advancement criteria were satisfied, the estimated performance values could then go beyond the 25 percent milestone.

This was a simple but effective way to measure project performance, and incorporated the best of (subjective) manager percent-complete estimates with specific (tangible) milestones that had predefined standards in order to satisfy. This approach still required the contribution of senior management as "checks" on the estimated values, in order to challenge excessive percent-complete estimates and to assure that no "gaming" was being done in the completion of milestone criteria. This approach worked well.

Case #2: CAPs for an Architectural Design Project

Shown in Figure 8.5 is a second example of a CAP; this one used "weighted milestones" to manage the performance of an architectural design subcontract in the construction sector. This CAP was used to monitor the performance of a subcontractor working on a cost-reimbursable-type contract that had a fixed fee, and then to authorize the release of fee payments to the supplier, based on its performance against specific-value milestones.

Prior to the award of the contract, the prime contractor and the subcontractor jointly met and agreed on the total design effort, and then subdivided the 100 percent contract value into nine discrete measurable pieces, each represented by specific completion milestones. Each milestone had predefined criteria to be achieved in order to be considered complete, and each was given a fixed performance value, as displayed in Figure 8.5. For simplicity of administration, they rounded each milestone to the closest 10 percent value.

This approach was simple, and yet it worked well. Earned value does not have to be a complicated process.

Case #3: CAPs for a Software Project

We now approach an area that is perhaps the new frontier for project management: software projects. How can one measure the performance of something that cannot be precisely defined? A reasonable question. One possible approach is to define in detail that portion of a new project that is possible to quantify, and leave the remaining undefined work in gross planning packages. In these cases, management will make a preliminary commitment to a new project, until the project can be reasonably quantified.

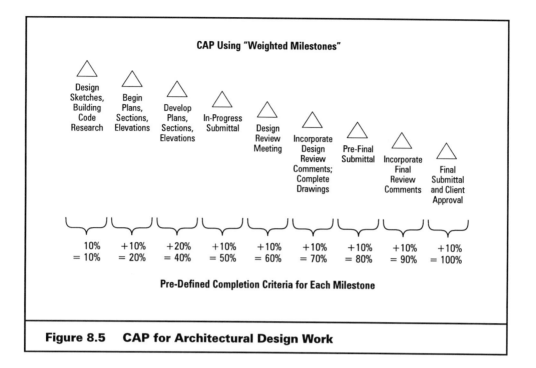

Figure 8.5   CAP for Architectural Design Work

Shown in Figure 8.6 is a third example of a project employing earned value, this one containing six CAPs to manage the performance of a software project. This same software project was previously defined with the WBS in Figure 5.7. While the total project will be budgeted within the six CAPs, as listed, only the first two CAPs will be planned in detail. The four remaining CAPs will be planned in detail later, but only after the project's requirements have been defined and subsequently analyzed.

For both of the two initially defined CAPs, a combination of subjective percent-completion estimates will be employed, but with use of specific milestones as gates. Each milestone, in order to be completed, must satisfy specific criteria that will be defined in advance of starting the work. The subjective estimates of percent complete cannot go past any milestone until that milestone is completed.

Note that the first CAP in Figure 8.6, covering "Requirements Definition," used four milestone gates at the 25%, 50%, 75%, and 100% points. Compare this with the second CAP, covering "Analysis of Requirements," which used only three milestones at 35%, 70%, and 100%. It is up to the CAP manager, working closely with the cost estimators, to set reasonable values for each milestone gate. Obviously, the project manager will want to review and approve each CAP prior to authorizing work to commence.

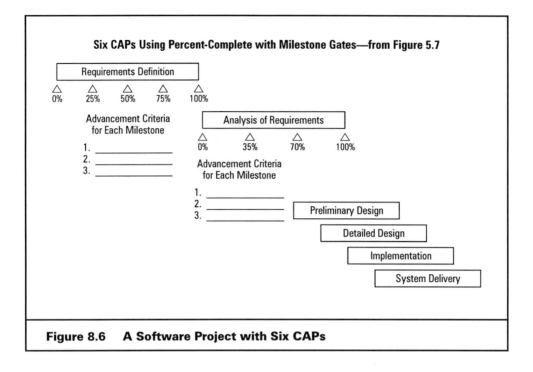

Figure 8.6   A Software Project with Six CAPs

This is an example of a software project employing a simple form of earned value, measuring that effort that can be defined up to the point where the total project can be quantified. A simple but effective form of earned value.

The Performance Measurement Baseline (PMB)

The PMB is an essential component of earned value project management. The PMB is the reference point against which a project will relate its actual accomplished work. It will tell the project whether it is keeping up with its planned schedule, and how much work is being accomplished in relation to the monies being spent. While the PMB is critical to the measurement of earned value performance, not all PMBs are alike. We need to understand this distinction.

The primary question: What is the composition of the PMB? Answer: It all depends on the particular company. The primary issue: For what does (senior) company management hold its project managers responsible in the area of cost performance. Our unofficial findings: The responsibilities of project managers for cost management vary considerably from one company to another company, and even from project to project within the same company. There are no absolute conditions that apply universally.

1. Direct Labor Hours (only)

2. Direct Labor Hours (within specific labor categories)

3. Direct Labor Costs (both hours and dollars)

4. Direct Labor in Total (through overhead applications)

5. Materials and Subcontract Costs

6. Other Direct Costs—ODC (e.g., travel)

7. All Project Costs (through general and adminstrative)

8. All Project Costs (including profit) = Contract Price

Figure 8.7   Composition of a PMB

Project managers are often held accountable for differing levels of cost performance on their projects. Thus, what constitutes a PMB for one project may be different from the PMB on another project, even within the same company.

To illustrate this point, we have attempted to define a spectrum of cost responsibilities for project managers, as shown in Figure 8.7. This figure begins with the more limited responsibilities as with item #1, where the project manager is charged with controlling only direct labor hours ... period. In many organizations, project managers will be charged with managing only direct labor hours; thus, their project PMBs will be composed purely of direct labor hours. While someone in the organization (likely finance) will need to convert the direct labor hours into dollars, here it is not the responsibility of the project manager.

With each additional step, the responsibilities of the project managers are broadened, and they are held accountable for managing additional categories of costs—as with overheads, materials, other direct costs, even profits. Total accountability for all profit and loss of a given project is shown with item #8 in Figure 8.7.

Many project managers will have limited responsibility managing all categories of project costs; thus, their performance baselines will be represented by the lower numbers, as illustrated in Figure 8.7. Other project managers will be charged with greater roles. However, in order to track earned value performance, we must understand precisely what management expects them to control.

Perhaps a couple of specific examples will help illustrate the point that we are making. We will display two examples of a PMB, one for a simple

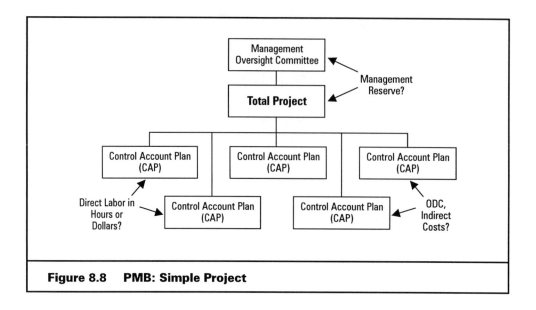

Figure 8.8   PMB: Simple Project

project, as illustrated in Figure 8.8, and another on a complex project, as in Figure 8.9.

Likely, the majority of projects can employ a simple earned value baseline, as illustrated in Figure 8.8. Here the project manager has divided the project into five points of management control, represented by the five CAPs.

Each CAP will contain a specific set of work to be accomplished, an authorized budget to accomplish the work, and a time frame for completing the work. Each CAP may be comprised of simply direct labor hours, as item #1 from Figure 8.7, or hours within labor categories, per item #2, and so forth. The PMB for this simple project will be composed of whatever categories of costs management expects the project manager to control. These CAPs may also include other direct cost items (ODC)—for example, materials, subcontracts, travel, and even indirect costs. It is always a good practice to separate labor from ODC.

What about a category of costs called Management Reserves (MR)? Again, there are no universal rules for us to follow. In some cases, senior management will allow the project manager to have and control MR; in other cases, senior management will want to control MR. Our recommendation is that, if the project manager owns some MR, that they be placed in a separate CAP strictly controlled by the project manager and not left in the various CAPs where likely it will be consumed.

To illustrate the PMB for a more complex type of project, quite often representing an external company contract being done for profit, refer to

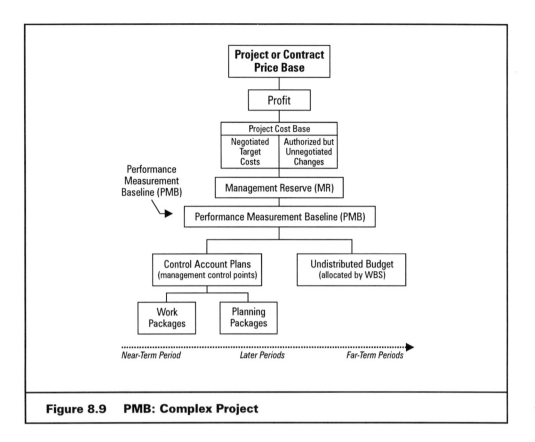

Figure 8.9   PMB: Complex Project

Figure 8.9. Here the project is progressively subdivided into various categories of costs, beginning with the total project or contract price base. After dedication of the anticipated profits by the chief financial officer, the project manager is left with the project cost base.

The project cost base is that value that the project manager has to manage for the project. It will include all categories of both direct and indirect project costs, even though the indirect costs will be beyond the immediate control of the project manager. Nevertheless, the project cost base must provide for all project costs, except for any forecasted profits.

One important issue that always exists for project managers is the necessary division of the authorized project cost base into two distinct parts: 1) those project costs that have been negotiated, and 2) those changes that have been authorized but not yet negotiated. In order to keep the project cost baseline consistent with a changing environment, the PMB must include both the negotiated scope and that effort that is recognized as a legitimate change, but the exact value of which has not been settled. Deciding precisely what value to budget for the authorized but unnegotiated work is always a challenge for the project manager. However, all authorized changes must be included in the project's performance baseline in order to maintain the integrity of the work being measured.

The PMB is displayed at the center of Figure 8.9 and is central to the earned value management process. Within the PMB will be housed two categories of budgets: the allocated budgets taking the form of CAPs, and the Undistributed Budgets (UBs) for the far-term periods, often represented by authorized but unnegotiated changes.

While UBs will reside at a higher summary planning level, such budgets need to be allocated to a specific element of the project WBS. Until UBs move into definitive CAPs, they may or may not be allocated to specific organizations for performance. However, all budgets within the PMB must be allocated to a specific WBS element and properly time-phased in order to maintain the integrity of the PMB.

The CAPs will be represented by two distinct categories: detailed work packages for the near-term effort, and gross planning packages for the distant work. There are no absolute rules for making the distinction between what constitutes a work package versus a planning package, or even UBs. These somewhat general categories will vary by project.

However, employing the "rolling wave" planning concept, projects with a duration of up to three years may well plan all of their CAPs to the work-package level. Other projects exceeding perhaps three years in duration may define their near-term effort in definitive work packages, but leave their out-year tasks in higher-level planning packages until they approach the period of performance. Projects with less than a five-year duration may have no use for UBs, except to temporarily house any authorized but not yet negotiated changes in scope.

Once the PMB has been established, based on individual CAPs, the next appropriate action is to time-phase the baseline to form a total project performance curve, as displayed in Figure 8.10. In this display, we have illustrated a project baseline of sufficient duration to warrant the use of both definitive work packages for the near term and planning packaged for the far-term effort.

Maintaining the Baseline: Managing Changes in Scope

A wise person is alleged to have said once: "There are three certainties in life: taxes, death, and changes to project scope." That wise individual must have worked on projects similar to ones that we have all enjoyed.

It is always frustrating to work hard to establish a project baseline, to have all parties agree on the baseline, and then watch the changes begin.

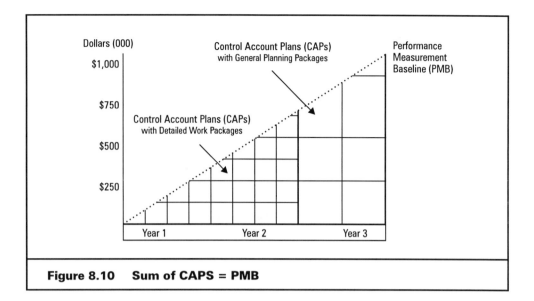

Figure 8.10   Sum of CAPS = PMB

Likely, it would not be possible to eliminate all changes, even if we could. Changes to project scope often result from a desire to make improvements in the final product deliverables. But if we cannot eliminate changes altogether, then at least we must strive to control the changes. Changes should represent what we intend to do, and not simply what we were unable to avoid.

Setting a firm baseline in place, based on an agreed-to scope of work, likely is a key initial action required by all project teams. Closely aligned to this task is for the project manager to have in place some type of change-control procedure that will allow the project to approve or reject changes, based on deliberate determination by the team. Changes in work scope should not inadvertently happen because someone failed to prevent them. Rather, scope changes should only result when specifically approved by one authorized to make changes ... the project manager.

In order to manage changes, a project needs to keep track of all pressures that it has encountered to change direction, deliberately or inadvertently. Controlling a baseline requires both information and an information retrieval system. Each action that alters or potentially alters the approved baseline needs to be carefully tracked, so that the project manager may make a conscious decision to approve or reject each change.

Shown in Figure 8.11 is a simple baseline change-control log. The first line item on such a log would be the initial approved project-baseline value. The next lines are reserved for change traffic, to be listed in chronological

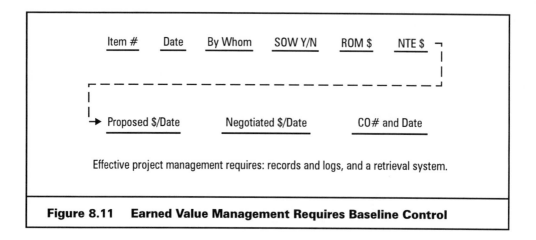

Item #	Date	By Whom	SOW Y/N	ROM $	NTE $

Proposed $/Date   Negotiated $/Date   CO# and Date

Effective project management requires: records and logs, and a retrieval system.

Figure 8.11   Earned Value Management Requires Baseline Control

order as they occur. Each change or potential change, as it surfaces, must be listed as a line item on the log.

As each potential change develops, the information will need to be systematically added to the log as it becomes available. For example, the rough order-of-magnitude (ROM) dollars need to be estimated and logged, and the authorized not-to-exceed (NTE) dollars need to be shown, leading ultimately to a negotiated amount and resulting change order (CO) being issued.

Effective project management requires that records and logs be kept, and that some type of information-retrieval system be put into place and maintained. Any of the automated spreadsheets or databases can facilitate this critical task for the project.

In Summary

Creating a detailed, bottoms-up project plan is needed in order to employ the earned value concept. Such plans need to be built upon detailed and individually measurable CAPs, the sum of which will form a project's time-phased PMB. Performance measurement takes place not at the top project level, but rather within each of the detailed CAPs.

Managing all changes to the project scope as they occur is essential to maintaining the approved project baseline, and is necessary to employ the earned value concept.

Chapter 9

Monitoring Performance against the Baseline

An Earned Value Performance Measurement (EVPM) baseline will now be in place for the project. The project's baseline will be formed by the creation of detailed Control Account Plans (CAPs), a generic form of management control cell. CAPs could best be thought of as a type of subproject. Thus, the sum of the subprojects, or CAPs, adds to the total project baseline.

To be viable, each CAP must have a defined scope of work typically in the form of work tasks, a time frame to start and finish each task, and an authorization for the required resources—that is, an approved budget. Each CAP will be performed and measured separately, and the sum of all CAPs will constitute the total project value.

The next step is for the project manager to monitor progress against the performance measurement baseline. Management will need to assess the long-term trends in project performance, and take any actions required to maintain its planned course. Earned value is a sort of strategic trend indicator, providing answers to a number of questions. For example, if the project were to continue at the present rate of performance, where will it end up? Based on the detailed plans and performance to them, how much money will be needed to complete the full project? How long will it take to complete the full project?

The purposes of EVPM are to discern the long-term performance direction of the project and to forecast its ultimate cost and schedule position, based on actual periodic performance.

Earned Value Focuses on "Exceptions" to the Plan

Although an earned value baseline will be created from the bottom-up, based on the sum of detailed CAPs, it does not require that each and every CAP be personally monitored by the project manager throughout the life of the project. Rather, the project manager and the team will simply focus their attention on exceptions to the baseline plan. Earned value is a "management-by-exception" technique.

Earned value allows the project manager and corporate executives to utilize the exceptions principle. It provides a sort of "50,000-foot observation platform" for busy executives to monitor the long-term performance trends of their projects taking the form of cost and schedule performance indices. Somewhat analogous to the "critical path" and "float" positions, earned value provides reliable indices to determine how much money and how much time it will take to finish the job.

Earned value performance can be numerically quantified and then displayed graphically for management oversight. Perfect performance for an earned value project is considered to be 1.0 performance, reflecting both the cost and schedule position. Any cost or schedule performance that runs below the 1.0 standard should receive the close scrutiny of the project manager, and perhaps even executive management. Earned value measurement can be expressed in dollars, hours, units, or in any measurable form. For simplicity, we will typically use dollars in our illustrations.

For example, perfect schedule performance to a project baseline will result in a dollar's worth of earned value being achieved for every dollar that was originally scheduled. Perfect schedule performance to its plan could thus be described as 1.0 performance. Anything less than 1.0 reflects a behind-schedule condition to the originally planned (scheduled) work.

On the cost side, one looks to the value of physical work that was actually accomplished (the earned value) as compared to the costs that were incurred for doing that same work. For every dollar of earned value achieved, only a dollar should have been spent; thus, the project would be performing at a cost efficiency factor of 1.0. It typically doesn't get better than 1.0 performance for earned value projects, although it may be mathematically possible. If, however, a project accomplishes less than a dollar's worth of physical earned value for every dollar that it spends, obviously the project will be experiencing a cost overrun for the work it has accomplished.

Unfortunately, actual performance sometimes falls below the 1.0 threshold, which sends a "buzzer" to the project, indicating that something is wrong. Once the project reflects earned value performance falling below

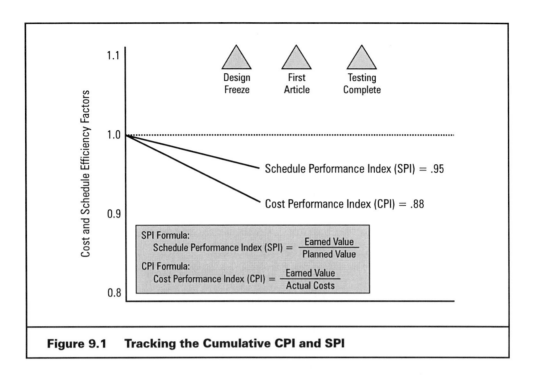

Figure 9.1   Tracking the Cumulative CPI and SPI

the 1.0 level for either the cost or scheduled work, the project management team will want to first understand the reasons causing the condition, and then take corrective actions to alter and improve performance on the remaining tasks.

Earned value projects have two areas of primary focus. The first is on the performance to the planned schedule. How much actual earned value was accomplished against the original planned value? To quantify this factor, the earned value accomplished is divided by the planned value, which provides what is called the Schedule Performance Index, or SPI. The SPI is a representation of how much of the original scheduled work has been accomplished at a particular point in time. The cumulative SPI position for a project can be quickly charted, as illustrated in Figure 9.1. It is a reflection of the work being done according to plan, or falling behind the plan. The formula for the SPI is reflected in the box at the bottom in Figure 9.1.

An SPI performance of less than 1.0 indicates that the project is running behind the dollar value of the work that it set out to accomplish. The earned value SPI when compared to the critical path method schedule position provides the project team with an accurate insight as to the true schedule position of the project. The earned value SPI and the critical path position, when used together, provide a means to accurately forecast how long the project will take to complete.

The second area of focus is that of cost performance. It represents that delicate relationship between the dollar value of the earned value physically accomplished versus the actual costs incurred to accomplish the work. This factor is called the Cost Performance Index (CPI), and cumulative cost performance position, together with the formula for creating the CPI, are also shown in Figure 9.1.

Both the SPI and CPI are important indicators to watch, but the CPI is clearly the more sensitive factor. The reason: A negative CPI position (less than 1.0) is likely to be nonrecoverable by the project. Whereas the SPI will eventually drift back up to a full 1.0 position when all of the project tasks have been completed, any CPI performance of less than 1.0 will rarely (perhaps never) be improved by the project. Thus, it is imperative that the project manager monitor closely the trend and rate of the cumulative CPI, as well as the completion of all those tasks that are on the critical path. The SPI is important during perhaps the early phases of a project, but becomes less significant as the project nears completion.

By contrast, overruns—meaning performance at less than a CPI of 1.0—will typically constitute a permanent loss of funds to the project. The only issue is at what rate the project will perform the remaining work: at the full budgeted value of 1.0 or at a lesser rate. There is strong empirical evidence suggesting that projects will most likely continue to perform at their "cumulative" CPI rate for all remaining tasks, and sometimes they will even deteriorate further. Only with the recognition that there is a cost problem, and through the aggressive management of all remaining tasks, can there ever be an improvement in the CPI position. Empirical evidence also suggests that while overruns can be improved by the project, they cannot be recovered in total.

The performance of any project that employs earned value can be effectively tracked with a focus on simply the cumulative CPI and SPI curves, as displayed in Figure 9.1. This chart reflects both the SPI and CPI curves over a time scale, with three key project milestones displayed across the top of the chart. Note that we recommend the use of cumulative data over monthly (or weekly) incremental data when monitoring earned value performance. Monthly or weekly incremental data are typically prone to wide fluctuations caused simply by the placement of planned or actual costs put into the wrong time frame. Cumulative data tends to smooth out such variances. More important, cumulative cost performance data has been demonstrated to be extremely accurate as forecasting tools with earned value projects.

The monitoring of cumulative SPI and CPI performance curves can be an effective management oversight tool. As illustrated in Figure 9.1, we have a project off to a bad start. Both the SPI and CPI curves are running in a negative direction. Let us attempt to describe what often happens on such projects, because it points out a common mistake.

Fact: Nobody likes to be behind schedule. Project managers in particular are sensitive to this condition. Therefore, in an attempt to get back on the planned schedule—that is, to bring their cumulative SPI back closer to a 1.0 performance position—project managers will often add resources to accomplish the same amount of budgeted work. The added resources may take the form of additional people, or sometimes paid overtime for the existing work force, or sometimes both. The battle cry is sounded: *Everyone on overtime!* Either way, the project will be consuming additional resources, but only to accomplish the same amount of planned value work. This reaction by management will cause a permanent overrun to project costs.

While the project team may dramatically improve the performance of its SPI, it will be doing nonrecoverable damage to its CPI position. Remember the rule: The SPI will eventually correct itself back to a full 1.0 when all the tasks have been completed. But any funds spent that cause an overrun inflict permanent damage to the CPI and cannot be subsequently recovered. Rather than the indiscriminate use of overtime, the project might better focus on the aggressive management of all late tasks along its critical path, and let the SPI eventually recover over time. Any project that is operating with limited funds—and most are—must maintain a careful balance between its SPI position and critical path schedule position, along with achieving its cost objectives.

The additional benefit in isolating the earned value SPI and CPI efficiency factors is that these two indices can be used to statistically forecast the estimated final costs for the project. Forecasting the final estimated costs for the project will be covered in our next chapter.

Performance Takes Place within CAPs

When the earned value concept was first introduced to the public in 1967, the point of management control was defined as the intersection between the lowest element of the Work Breakdown Structure (WBS) with a single functional organization. These points were initially called Cost Account Plans, later changed to Control Account Plans, both called CAPs. The combination of the lowest WBS element and a single function resulted in the creation of an excessive number of CAPs, too many for effective management use. Within these specified CAPs would take place all EVPM.

The initial creation and subsequent maintenance of detailed CAPs require discipline from everyone on the project, and this sometimes presents a challenge. Each of the authorized CAPs must be carefully maintained, meaning that the specified scope of work and its corresponding budget must remain in concert. Once authorized, neither the defined scope (by itself) nor the corresponding budget (by itself) can be shifted, independent of the other. Indiscriminate shifts in either budget or scope would serve to distort the performance within CAPs, and negate the very purpose of employing earned value.

While having performance measurement take place at the detailed CAP level, the project manager may monitor periodic (typically weekly or monthly) performance at three levels, as depicted in Figure 9.2. Thus, project performance may be tracked: 1) within the individual CAPs, 2) at some intermediate summary level, reflecting either a WBS element or a functional Organizational Breakdown Structure (OBS) level, and 3) at the top project level. Each of these three levels will reflect an individual performance pattern that can be used to discern the periodic or cumulative trends, as well as to forecast a final position.

The project manager and the customer typically will have a particular interest in monitoring project performance by WBS element, with a focus on any high-cost or high-risk elements. By contrast, internal functional management will typically center its attention on the performance of its respective functional departments. Functions that happen earliest will receive the closest initial scrutiny—for example, engineering design.

Three decades ago, when earned value was introduced, the use of small, short-span CAPs was in vogue. This approach resulted in the formation of huge numbers of detailed CAPs, an excessive number for projects to monitor. More recently, and consistent with the increased popularity of using multifunctional project teams, there has been a major attitudinal change within the earned value community. Typically, we now see larger homogenous groupings of (WBS) work effort being defined as the CAPs, while incorporating all of the multifunctions necessary to perform the work.

The multifunctional CAP has resulted in a higher-level placement of defined work on the WBS—that is, larger segments of homogeneous work. This is a more logical approach to work definition and has resulted in a major reduction in the total number of required CAPs for any project. The

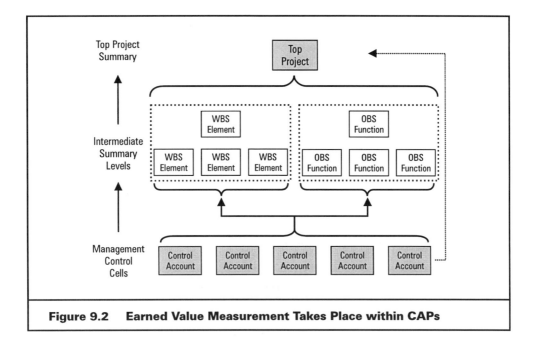

Figure 9.2   Earned Value Measurement Takes Place within CAPs

multifunctional CAP also represents a more natural subdivision of project work, which seems to have gained better acceptance from all parties.

There is nothing inherently wrong with utilizing larger segments of defined work as CAPs as long as these units represent a definitive scope of work, expressed in discrete work tasks, each containing its own budget and schedule. Performance measurement will not be compromised with larger, but less, CAPs per project.

Displays for Management

Management needs to be kept informed on how well or how poorly each project is performing. Two of the more illuminating presentations of earned value performance are best displayed in a side-by-side format, as shown in Figure 9.3.

On the left side of Figure 9.3 is a display of cumulative performance data representing the three key elements of the planned value, the actual costs, and, of course, the earned value. This likely is the most popular of all earned value displays. Management can step back and quickly assess the long-term trend in project performance. And when the major project milestones are depicted across the top of the display, this chart becomes a very effective tool for all levels of management: project, executive, functional, the customer, and so on.

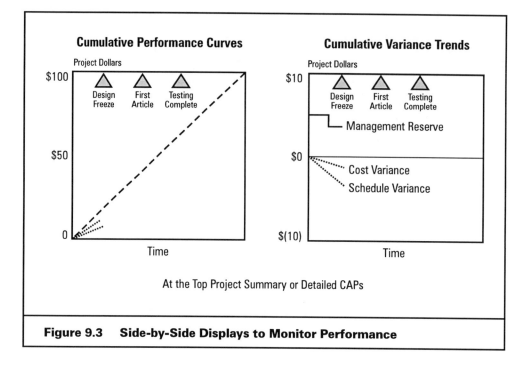

Figure 9.3   Side-by-Side Displays to Monitor Performance

And as a complement to the cumulative performance curve shown on the left, the resulting cost and schedule performance variances can be magnified for closer examination, as displayed on the right side of Figure 9.3. Both charts are depicted with use of a common horizontal time scale and common project milestones, but the cost and schedule variances on the right explode the data with use of a smaller time scale. In addition, the project's initial management reserve and its consumption can be tracked on the variance chart to the right. Thus, in these two side-by-side displays, a wealth of performance data can be observed quickly by the project manager.

These same side-by side displays can reflect earned value project data at various levels. Figure 9.2 displays three levels of project activity: the detailed CAPS, the intermediate WBS or OBS summaries, and the top project summary. Side-by-side charts can reflect data at all levels of earned value projects.

How is this project doing? Obviously, unless there is a dramatic improvement in earned value performance, one can quickly see that the project will take longer than originally planned, and cost more than the current authorized budget. It is time for aggressive management actions to be taken on all of the remaining project work tasks.

Using an earned value technique, with its focus on "exceptions" to the baseline plan, the project manager knows exactly when actions must be taken to improve performance for the remaining work. By monitoring the top project performance with use of the two displays, as illustrated in Figure 9.3, management can quickly tell when the project is veering from an acceptable direction. The project manager can immediately "drill down" to focus attention on the individual CAPs that are causing the problems observed at the top displays. They know exactly where the corrective actions must take place.

The utility of earned value is that these "early warning" signals can be observed as early as 15 to 20 percent into the project's performance cycle … in adequate time to take corrective actions for all remaining tasks to change the final outcome.

Special Issue: The Meaning of Earned Value Schedule Variances

It often comes as a surprise to many that what is called the "Schedule Variance" (SV) on an earned value project is in fact *not* a true SV. Rather the earned value SV simply reflects a variance from the approved baseline plan!

A negative SV in earned value simply means that the project has fallen behind in accomplishing its planned work. Conversely, a positive SV simply means that the project is ahead of the work that it initially planned to do. It is sometimes deceiving to look at an earned value schedule position alone, and to rely on it for providing the project's schedule position. Projects need other scheduling tools with measurement metrics to discern their true schedule position. Confusing? We hope not.

In the mid-1980s, the Department of Defense (DOD) commissioned the prestigious consulting firm of Arthur D. Little to study the earned value concept and report back to the DOD on its findings. This firm described the meaning of earned value SVs about as well as any that we have heard. We will quote two sentences from its final report to the DOD, inserting the term "earned value" before "C/SCSC," as it was then called:

> An [earned value] C/SCSC schedule variance is stated in terms of dollars of work and must be analyzed in conjunction with other schedule information such as provided by networks, Gantt charts, and line-of-balance.

> By itself, the [earned value] C/SCSC schedule variance reveals no "critical path" information, and may be misleading because unfavorable accomplishments in some areas can be offset by favorable accomplishments in others (Arthur D. Little Company 1986).

Whenever a project is employing earned value and it experiences a negative schedule condition, it should analyze the meaning of this condition, as depicted in Figure 9.4. In this figure, a project has fallen behind in accomplishing its planned work; that is, it is running a schedule position of less than 1.0. Recommendation: Those tasks that are late to the original plan should be carefully reviewed to determine two things.

First issue: Are the late tasks on the critical path, or on the near critical paths, so as to delay the final completion of the project? Second issue: Are the late tasks considered high risks to the project; that is, do they constitute a risk of not meeting project objectives? If either of these conditions exists, then those tasks that are on the critical path or are high risks to the project must be completed at the earliest possible date. Overtime and added resources may be in order to complete these critical tasks at the earliest time.

If however, these late-to-plan tasks are determined to have positive schedule float position (or slack) and are not felt to be high risks, then added resources should not be allotted. The reason: added resources will only have a negative impact on the cost efficiency rate, and produce no positive (critical path) schedule results.

Special Issue: Accounting for Materials and Subcontracts

It is fairly easy to measure earned value performance on direct labor. Most firms today have good labor-reporting systems that allow for the measurement of their planned value and earned value, and for reporting actual labor hours or dollars. Even indirect burdens can be tracked fairly easily, because they typically are merely a function of direct labor costs.

However, we will now discuss a challenging (perhaps even ugly) subject for earned value: how to measure the performance of the items that we buy from other companies. These are procured items and can represent a range of deliverables from simple on-the-shelf articles to complex new parts being made to our specifications. These items come to us as a result of our issuing a simple purchase order, contract, or, sometimes, subcontract.

Any project that measures its earned value must be capable of continuously monitoring two critical performance variances resulting from three points of measured data: planned value, earned value, and actual costs for the earned value. The first required relationship is the Schedule Variance

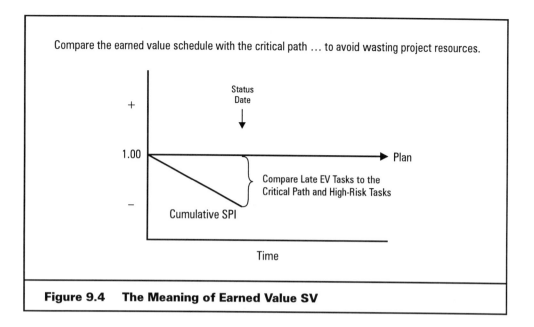

Compare the earned value schedule with the critical path … to avoid wasting project resources.

Figure 9.4   The Meaning of Earned Value SV

(SV), the difference between the earned value less the planned value. The second relationship is the Cost Variance (CV), the difference between the earned value less the actual costs incurred to achieve the earned value. Both variances are depicted in Figure 9.5. In order to measure these variances, one must be able to synchronize measurements of these three relationships: planned value, earned value, and actual costs.

The SV is an important relationship to monitor, but only during the period of project performance. Eventually the SV will go away, as all the planned work has been completed or earned. It is a fairly easy process to measure, since both the planned value and the earned value are embedded within the project's scheduling system. The actual measurement of earned value should always be accomplished using the same tangible metrics as were used to develop the original planned value.

However, the measurement of the project's CV is a different matter. The CV consists of that relationship between the earned value achieved less the actual costs consumed to accomplish the earned value. The CV is the more critical of the two relationships because poor cost performance is normally nonrecoverable for the work performed. If one overruns the costs for completed work, it will likely not be offset by performance on subsequent tasks.

Measuring the actual costs for the earned value of materials and subcontracts is more difficult than it may first seem. The actual costs that are recorded on the company's general ledger may not support the measurement

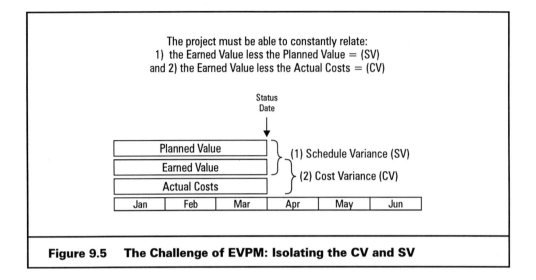

Figure 9.5   The Challenge of EVPM: Isolating the CV and SV

process. The actual costs on the books may well be too little (understated) or too much (overstated) for the earned value being measured. Rarely are actual costs on the books precisely in synch with the measured earned value.

However difficult to achieve, purchased materials and subcontracts must be accurately measured, simply because they sometimes represent a sizable portion of the total project budget. But it will not be easy. Some examples: the accounting commitment for materials, the placement of the actual order for materials, the receipt of the physical goods, the ultimate consumption of the materials, and the subsequent payment to the supplier may well all take place in different time periods. How does one measure earned value performance when the planned value, the earned value, and actual costs occur in different time frames?

Let us discuss the issue from two extremes. Costs on the books are either overstated or understated and must be adjusted in order to match the earned value measured. Figure 9.6 attempts to illustrate these conditions.

Actual Costs May Need to be Reduced to Match Earned Value Measurement

In the construction industry, it is not uncommon to use some type of an "advance" or "mobilization payment" by an owner to aid the performing constructor of a new project. The purpose and timing of such payments must be determined in order to synchronize the physical earned value performance with the actual recorded costs. If such advance payments were to be used strictly for the mobilization of construction forces, and such work

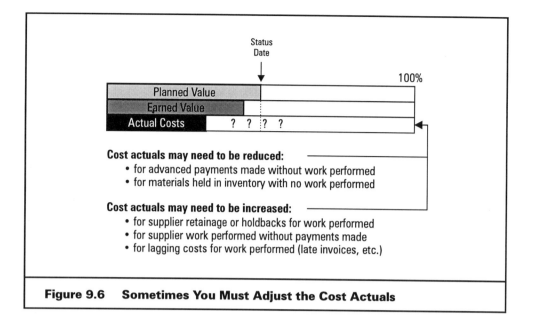

Figure 9.6   Sometimes You Must Adjust the Cost Actuals

would take place within a short time period—that is, within the period being measured—then a separate task, labeled "mobilization," may be planned and performed, and the actual costs incurred during a single measured time frame. The three relationships thus would be synchronized.

If, however, the advanced payment is to be used partially for mobilization and partly to aid the constructor with its initial cash flow, then the two activities must be divided into two separate work tasks in order to relate the payments to the physical work being measured. This would be particularly true if the cash-flow credits were to extend over several months before repayment of funds back to the owner. Two work packages must be established and measured separately: 1) contractor mobilization, perhaps a one-month task, and 2) cash-flow advance, perhaps performed over six months.

A second condition of (temporary) overpayment may occur whenever the project purchases materials, some of which may be immediately used on the project, and some of which may be put into the project inventory and possibly later transferred to another separate project. It is not uncommon to buy materials for multiple projects but, for convenience, charge the costs and store the materials on a single project. However, such practices will distort the measurement of performance on any given project. Solution: The surplus or inventoried materials must be separated into a separate work package so that both the performance and actual costs may be applied against the proper project.

Actual Costs May Need to Be Increased to Match Earned Value Measurement

Sometimes the very opposite condition may occur with materials and subcontracts. Performance for materials and subcontracts may be monitored and properly claimed, but the actual costs for the earned value may not be fully recorded on the project's cost ledger. How does this happen? The bottom of Figure 9.6 relates the situation.

Returning once again to the construction industry—which seems to monitor its supplier's performance as well as any industry—in order for a supplier to be paid progress payments for construction work, the supplier must demonstrate that it has physically performed the work. Sounds a little like earned value, and it is, but the cost engineers in the construction industry typically do not call it such.

The performing supplier must define the job in the form of detailed subtasks, with a value assigned to each task, the sum of which must total the costs of the subcontract. It typically calls this a "schedule of values." In order to be paid for the work, the subcontractor must carefully estimate the value of the work accomplished for each task. It sets the percentage complete, the earned value for each task.

Assume that the total construction subcontract has a total value of $1,000,000. After the first month, the supplier estimates that it is 10 percent complete with the total job, by individual task, or $100,000 complete. The project manager agrees with this estimate. A check for $100,000 is prepared, less what is called a "retention" or "withhold" amount of perhaps 10 percent, a holdback value that is common in construction-type work. The check would be for a net value of only $90,000.

Thus, if the project were measuring its earned value performance, it might claim $100,000 in the earned value for the supplier, but only $90,000 in actual costs would be on its cost ledger. Someone could easily draw the wrong conclusions with regard to the performance of this supplier. Someone could assume that the cost performance efficiency for this work is 1.11 ($100,000 in earned value divided by $90,000 actual costs = 1.11), which would be fictional cost performance. In fact, the subcontract should be running at 1.0 ($100,000 in earned value divided by $100,000 in actual costs = 1.0), at full value.

Eventually, when the retention is later paid to the supplier, the inflated cost performance will return to a correct position. In the meantime, however, the overvalued performance of the subcontracted work at a CPI of 1.11 may well serve to mask poor performance of other critical areas that may need the attention of the project manager. When the costs are rolled up to the top of the project, the distorted values of one control account may serve to offset the performance of another.

In order to reflect the proper values within all CAPs, the labor CAPs should be separated from the materials and subcontracted CAPs. If the material or subcontract CAPs are reflecting their full earned value performance, but the related cost actuals reflect only the net costs being paid to the supplier (payment less retentions), then the cost efficiency performance values (CPI) will be distorted. A simple accounting accrual or estimated value must be included for the holdback values in order to not distort the measurements being recorded. The actual cost values on the books for materials and subcontracts may need to be temporarily adjusted upward or downward to match the earned value being measured.

We said that materials and subcontracts would be an ugly subject, and it has been! But it is also critical to the fidelity of the performance measurement concept.

Chapter 10

Forecasting Final Cost and Schedule Results

There are numerous reasons why more and more companies are beginning to employ a simple form of earned value to help manage their projects. Earned value requires that projects work to an "integrated" baseline plan, meaning that the defined scope of work must relate to the authorized resources, which are then set into a time frame for performance. We know of no other technique that fully integrates the project's scope, costs, and schedules.

But perhaps the single most compelling reason to employ earned value is that it enables the project manager to be able to "statistically" forecast the (probable) final cost, and schedule results on the project ... from as early as the 15 percent completion point. With earned value, the project does not have to wait until it is 90 percent spent to know that it has a problem. The 90 percent point is too late to alter the project's final course. Earned value provides an "early warning" message to management in time to take corrective action, in time to influence the final results with aggressive action.

Shown in Figure 10.1 is an example of what we mean. The project has been defined, and a budget (BAC) authorized for the work. The project has completed only 15 percent of its work, but it is off to a bad start. Performance has not kept up with its scheduled plan, and it is spending more money to complete the work than it had budgeted. It is both behind schedule and experiencing an overrun. With an earned value baseline in place, the project can quickly forecast how much it will need in added resources and time to complete the total project. Earned value predicts the final performance results, providing a statistical range of values in time to take aggressive management actions.

Such early forecasts have proven to be extremely reliable using earned value data. They are based on a combination of two factors: 1) the implementation of a detailed bottoms-up performance plan, and then 2) the subsequent actual performance against the detailed project plan. These two factors have been shown to produce amazingly accurate statistical forecasts.

Two performance indices resulting from earned value are needed to forecast the project's final cost and schedule results. The first and most valuable is called the Cost Performance Index (CPI), which represents that delicate relationship between the value of the work physically completed and in process, related to the actual costs incurred for doing such work. If one spends more money than one physically performs, such performance results in an "overrun."

The second index needed to forecast final results is the Schedule Performance Index (SPI), which measures the work accomplished to the baseline plan. These two indices can be used independently or in conjunction to statistically predict the final results quickly and accurately.

Three Factors Will Determine the Final Project Results

While the earned value performance indices can be most useful in predicting the final results on any project, the utility of these indices are subject to three critical factors. Each of these factors deserves some discussion, because they can influence the utility of the performance indices in predicting the final cost and schedule outcome.

Factor #1: The Quality of the Project's Baseline Plan

Not all project plans are created equal. Some individuals and companies are quite good at preparing their project plans; others are not. Some people consistently "fire first" and "aim later." The quality of project plans will vary and influence the final project results.

The competitive environment under which a given project plan is implemented likely will influence or bias the project manager's strategy. Competition often results in risk-taking by the creators of the plans, and will incorporate varying degrees of risks into the final baseline plan. Project plans are often different, depending upon the amount of competition present when management gives its final approval. Earned value will

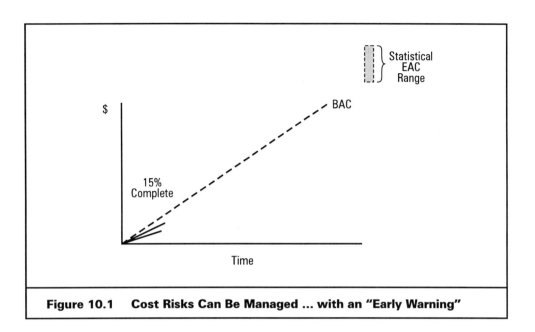

Figure 10.1   Cost Risks Can Be Managed ... with an "Early Warning"

measure performance to the baseline plan, whether the plan is realistic or otherwise.

The quickest way to experience "scope creep" is to not adequately define the initial project scope. The surest way to "overrun" project costs is to underbudget the project. The best way to assure a schedule slip is to dictate a completion date that is impossible to achieve. Earned value accurately measures project performance, but must assume that scope definition is adequate and that the project has been given an achievable budget and a realistic schedule.

Factor #2: Actual Performance against the Approved Baseline Plan

Once the project plan has been approved and implemented, another important variable will come into play. This variable is the actual performance results against the authorized plan. Is the project's performance meeting, exceeding, or falling behind the approved project plan? Such performance factors can be quantified and monitored for the duration of the project.

Both the CPI and the SPI efficiency factors, once established, can be monitored for trends and used to statistically forecast the final results for any project employing earned value.

Factor #3: Management's Determination to Influence the Final Results

A third factor is also most critical and can often influence the project's final results. If project management closely tracks its earned value performance trends and does not like, or cannot accept, the final forecasted results, then to what extent will management take aggressive actions on the remaining work to alter the final outcome?

Final forecasted results are not necessarily preordained. Final project results can often be altered, but only when aggressive management actions are taken. The critical variables are several. To what extent will project performance data be monitored and the data believed by management? What actions will be taken to alter the management approach on the remaining project tasks? And finally, if the project's final projects are unacceptable, to what extent will all discretionary work be eliminated, budgets reduced, risks taken, and so forth in order to bring the final projected results down to acceptable levels?

Aggressive project management actions, if taken early, can often alter the final projected outcome for the project.

Methodology to Statistically Forecast Final Cost and Schedule Results

As was discussed in the previous chapter (Chapter 9, Monitoring Performance against the Baseline), the actual results for any project employing earned value allows it to continuously monitor its cost and schedule efficiency rates, reflecting actual performance trends.

The first measurement is the actual performance against the planned schedule, or the physical accomplishment of the work scheduled. Has the project accomplished what it set out to do, and within the same time frame? This is a metric that can be quantified and measured against a performance standard of 1.0, as depicted in Figure 10.2. Perfect schedule performance is represented by one dollar of earned value accomplished for each one dollar of work planned.

The second and a closely related issue is that of cost performance. Cost efficiency can also be measured with use of a 1.0 performance standard, representing the relationship of earned value accomplished against the actual costs spent to do the work. This is also displayed in Figure 10.2, and the formulas for both these standards are shown in the two boxes at the bottom of the chart.

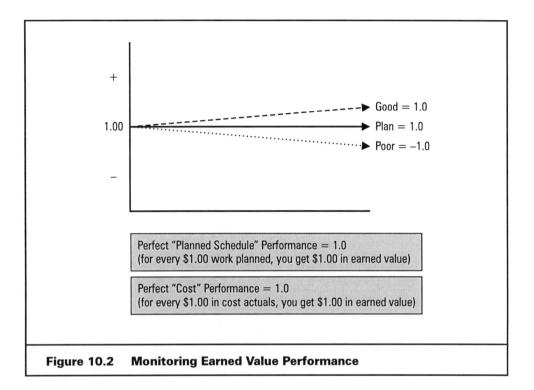

Figure 10.2   Monitoring Earned Value Performance

Over the years, there have been numerous formulas developed to statistically forecast the final Estimated Costs at Completion (EAC) on any project employing earned value. By last count, there were perhaps somewhere close to twenty distinct formulas available to predict the final cost position. We will limit our discussion to just three of the more accepted formulas.

With use of these three formulas, any project can continuously quantify a reliable range of final values from which to display the possible results. (**Important point**: We are not trying to pick a final forecasted number for the project; that task belongs to the project manager and is typically done with bottoms-up cost estimates, not with a statistical forecast. Rather, we are simply attempting to assess whether or not we have a cost problem that needs our immediate attention.)

The processes of statistically forecasting a range of final cost estimates will center on determining three variables for a project, as of any given point in time:

1. Take the total of actual costs incurred to date.
2. Then determine the value of the Work Remaining (WR), which is the budgeted value for the uncompleted tasks, typically expressed as the

total Budget at Completion (BAC), less the earned value already accomplished.

3. Divide the WR by some performance efficiency factor (for example: the cumulative CPI, or the CPI times SPI, or some combination of the two indices).

With these three variables, we can statistically forecast the final costs for the project.

Special Issue: Management Reserve or Contingency Reserve

An important issue for some projects when forecasting their final statistical financial position is: What do you do with Management Reserves (MR) or Contingency Reserves (CR) if such funds exist? Some projects do not have MR or CR because management will not authorize them for the project, so that this is a non-issue for many projects. However, if there are MR or CR funds available to the project manager, then they must be considered while making a final statistical cost projection.

One of three things can happen to MR or CR funds, which is an individual judgment call by the project manager:

1. The final EAC forecast can be reduced by the full value of the remaining MR or CR funds, which assumes that these funds will not be consumed.

2. The remaining MR or CR can be divided by some negative performance efficiency factor (CPI or CPI times SPI), which will increase the final projected costs.

3. The MR or CR can be added to the calculated EAC at its full 1.0 value, which assumes that these funds will be consumed, but at their full value.

Since the allocation of MR or CR typically goes for specific, well-defined tasks at the time that the budget is released, we would tend to support number 3, to add the full value of MR or CR to the EAC, but at its full 1.0 value.

Again, the consumption of MR or CR funds is a judgment call by the project manager.

The "Mathematical" or "Overrun to Date" EAC

The first of the three forecasting techniques to be discussed is called the "mathematical" or "overrun to date" EAC forecast. It is depicted in Figure 10.3, and its formula is displayed in the box at the bottom. The formula

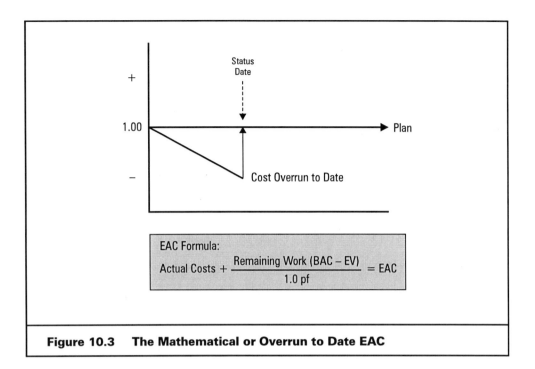

Figure 10.3   The Mathematical or Overrun to Date EAC

could have been shortened to simply: EAC = Actual Costs plus BAC less Earned Value (EV). However, in order to compare the three statistical EAC methods using the same format, we have used: Actual Costs plus the work remaining divided by a performance factor.

In this case, the performance factor employed is 1.0, which means that it assumes that all future work, starting tomorrow, will be done precisely at the full budgeted rate—an ambitious goal. This formula is not widely accepted in government quarters and has actually been called "useless." However, it is a frequently used formula within private industry for a couple of valid reasons.

First, the mathematical or overrun to date EAC is often the first display that announces to the project manager and executive management that they have a cost problem. As we discussed in Chapter 1, if a project spends $300,000 to accomplish only $200,000 of budgeted work, then the project has experienced an overrun for the work that it has performed. This formula assumes that, starting tomorrow, all future work will be accomplished at the fully budgeted value of 1.0.

Second, the mathematical EAC is important because an overrun to date does not go away with time. We have never witnessed an overrun to date disappear through exemplary performance of subsequent work. Think about it. Where is the best scope definition, the best planning, best budget, most realistic schedule placed in any project: in the first half or the last half of the project? Likely it will be in the first half. Thus, if a project incurs an overrun in the first half, what are the chances of making a later recovery of the overrun? Little to none.

Short of a project dropping features, descoping work, or the outright elimination of tasks, an overrun in the early phases of the project is likely to constitute a permanent loss of funds to any project. The mathematical or overrun to date EAC formula has utility in that it displays the lowest possible value in the range of possible final costs for any project.

The "Cumulative CPI" EAC

Likely, the most common and most respected of all such statistical forecasting techniques is displayed in Figure 10.4, The "cumulative CPI" EAC. The formula for this method is displayed at the bottom of the chart and incorporates the three variables described earlier. This formula has the most scientific data accumulated, supporting its reliability as a forecasting tool.

Note the emphasis on the use of only "cumulative performance" data, not periodic or incremental data. While any project will certainly want to monitor its periodic position to assess performance trends, period data are too subject to anomalies, typically caused by placing good data into the wrong time frame. Cumulative performance data tends to smooth these variations, but nevertheless retaining its value as a long-term forecasting tool.

The cumulative (not period) CPI provides a particularly reliable index to watch, because it has been demonstrated to be an accurate and reliable forecasting metric. The cumulative CPI has been shown to stabilize from as early as the 15 to 20 percent point in the project's percentage completion point. One particularly important scientific study described the value of using the cumulative CPI to forecast the final cost results on projects:

> Researchers found that the cumulative CPI does not change by more than 10 percent once a contract is 20 percent complete; in most cases, the cumulative CPI only worsens as a contract proceeds to completion (Christensen 1994).

Some people consider the cumulative CPI EAC formula to represent the very "minimum" in costs that the project will need to complete all its work. Others consider it to be the "most likely" final estimate of project costs. Either way, the cumulative CPI EAC has been demonstrated to be most accurate in providing a quick statistical forecast of the final project

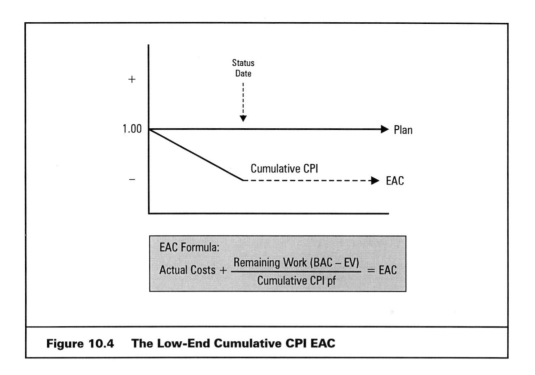

Figure 10.4   The Low-End Cumulative CPI EAC

costs. Such statistical forecasts, when compared against the "official" final estimate for any project, should never be ignored by the project manager or executive management.

Just how valid is this particular formula to the Department of Defense (DOD), who has been using earned value data to forecast final cost results for over three decades? In 1991, when the DOD moved the requirement for earned value management directly into its acquisition policy, it also required that the cumulative CPI be employed whenever forecasting the final costs:

> Provide the estimate at completion reflecting the best professional judgement of the servicing cost analysis organization. If the contract is at least 15 percent complete and the estimate is lower than that calculated using the cumulative cost performance index, provide an explanation. (United States DOD 1991).

There may be valid reasons supporting an EAC less than that calculated using the cumulative CPI. However, since 1991, all DOD project managers must describe how this will be accomplished. The cumulative CPI EAC forecast is a vital technique for all earned value projects.

The "Cumulative CPI times SPI" EAC

The last statistical formula that has wide professional acceptance in forecasting the final project costs is one that combines both the cost efficiency (CPI) factor and the schedule efficiency (SPI) factor. This method is displayed in Figure 10.5, and its formula is shown in the box at the bottom of the chart.

There is a solid rational basis to support the use of a forecasting formula that incorporates both the cost and the schedule dimensions. The reason: no project ever likes to be in a position of creating a performance plan, getting management approval, and then falling behind with its authorized plan. There is a natural human tendency to want to get back on schedule, even if it means consuming more resources to accomplish the same amount of work. Extensive use of paid overtime and additional resources are often employed, simply resulting in permanent, nonrecoverable cost damage to their most reliable efficiency factor, the CPI.

Some people consider this formula to be a "worst-case" scenario. Others consider it to be the "most likely" forecast. In either case, the CPI times the SPI EAC is one of the more widely used and accepted formulas to statistically forecast the high-end cost requirements for any project.

Question: What is the utility of providing a statistical range of final cost results for any project? Simply put, it is to test the reasonableness of the project manager's "official" cost forecast against the earned value statistical forecasts. Earned value forecasts can quickly provide management with a "range" of final cost EAC. If a given project displays the low-end formulas, as per Figures 10.3 or 10.4, against a high-end formula, as portrayed in Figure 10.5, it has effectively provided a "range" of final cost estimates to compare against other forecasted positions.

If the project manager is predicting final cost performance of the project outside of the statistical range, either above or below the range, then the basis for this position should be explained to all parties who have a vested interest in the project. Those vested-interest parties may be the project owner, senior executive management, corporate shareholders, and so forth.

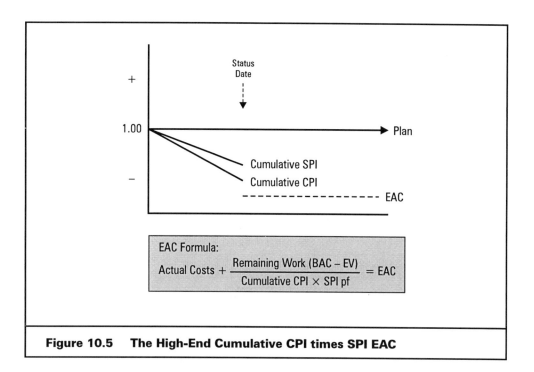

Figure 10.5   The High-End Cumulative CPI times SPI EAC

The To Complete (the Remaining Work) Performance Index

One additional method used by projects to monitor their earned value performance data needs discussion. It is a display that tells management precisely what performance factor must be achieved on the remaining work in order to stay within the financial goals set by management. Such financial goals can be variable and can represent the original project budget, a revised estimate, a contract ceiling, and so on. This formula is called the "To Complete (the remaining work) Performance Index (TCPI), and is shown in Figure 10.6. The formula is also shown in the box at the bottom, but note carefully that the denominator constitutes the "Funds Remaining," which can be a variable amount.

The TCPI is used to determine what cost performance factor will be needed to complete all remaining work according to some financial goal set by management. It simply takes the value of the "Remaining Work" and divides it by the value of the "Funds Remaining."

What-if scenarios can be explored to set realistic (or ambitious) financial goals for the project. The value for the funds remaining can be established for the project reflecting any of the following: 1) BAC, or the latest 2) EAC, or the 3) fixed price ceiling of a contract, or for any value, always, of course, less the actual costs that have been incurred to date.

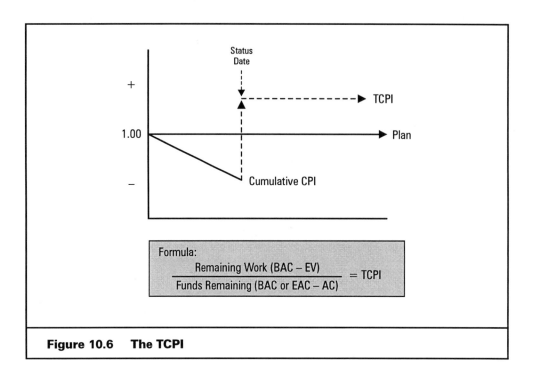

Figure 10.6   The TCPI

The formula for the TCPI is thus:

$$\frac{\textbf{Work Remaining} \text{ (BAC, less Earned Value)}}{\textbf{Funds Remaining} \text{ (BAC or latest EAC, less Actual Costs)}} = \text{TCPI}$$

Management at any level is quick to grasp the realities that when you are exactly halfway through the project and have achieved a cumulative performance factor of only .8, then the project, in order to stay within the budget goals, must achieve a performance factor of 1.2 for all remaining work. At some point, as such performance challenges continue to increase, become impossible, the realization of the cost overruns has to be acknowledged.

Predicting the Project's Time Duration

How long will it take to complete a project? This is another vital issue that is always of concern to the project manager, senior management, and especially the owner.

By definition, the project will be completed within the outer parameters of its critical path. The critical path for any project determines the shortest time frame for its completion. By definition, the critical path

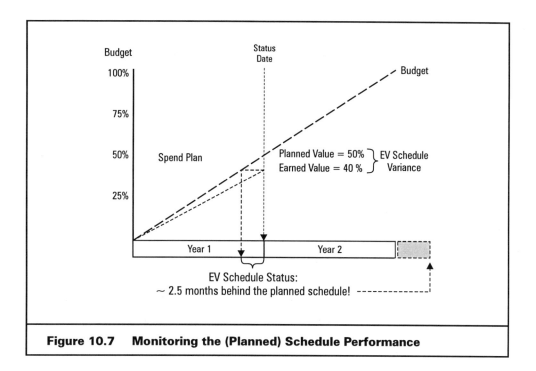

Figure 10.7   Monitoring the (Planned) Schedule Performance

represents "the longest sequential path of activities which are absolutely essential for completion of the project" (Lewis 1995).

Management of the project's critical path and the near-critical paths are vital to the successful completion of any project, at the earliest possible date.

In addition to closely monitoring the critical path, and as another way of predicting the final duration of the project, the earned value Schedule Variance (SV) position may be used in conjunction with the critical path as a way of reinforcing the forecasted date for project completion.

Displayed in Figure 10.7 is a chart that depicts the two elements of earned value dealing with schedule performance: the planned (schedule) value and the earned value accomplished. Such values may be expressed in monetary units, or, as in this example, percent-complete values. Any values that can be quantified will work.

As of the status date, halfway through a two-year project, the plan called for completion of 50 percent of the work, but had only accomplished 40 percent of the job. If we take the point of intersection of the earned value accomplished with the status date, and trace it backwards to the planned schedule value line, then move the line downward to the bottom time scale, then we can see that the project is running approximately two and one-half months behind the planned earned value schedule.

The comparison of the earned value SV with the management of the critical path simply reinforces the validity in prediction of how long it likely will take to complete the project. An accurate determination of the critical path position, used in conjunction with the earned value SV, will help the project manager forecast the final completion date for the project.

In Summary

The bottom-line questions for any project are typically how much will it cost to complete the job, and how much time until the project is over. Two reliable methods are currently available to any project manager: the use of the CPM and the earned value performance measurement technique.

While many projects today will employ the CPM to manage the time dimension for their projects, the use of earned value measurement has been somewhat limited. It is our belief that the two techniques work well together and are in fact complementary. When these two proven techniques are used by people working with a single integrated database, they can provide accurate and reliable forecasts to the age-old questions: How long will my project take to complete, and how much money will it cost?

Chapter 11

Reengineering the Earned Value Process for the Private Sector

We consider earned value to be an important tool in the management of our projects. In fact, at certain of our locations we have required earned value to be employed on all of our software projects over 2,000 hours in size.

Mahvash Yazdi, Senior Vice President and CIO,
Southern California Edison & Edison International

Earned value is used by our program office to identify activities which have adverse cost or schedule variances. This allows our projects to take corrective action so that the end date of the project and its budget are not impacted.

Melanie Thomas, PMP, Senior Manager, Project Support,
Computer Sciences Corporation, Tucson, Arizona

Exciting things are beginning to happen with earned value project management. Private industry is grabbing hold of the technique and transforming it into a valuable tool for all project managers. No longer is earned value considered a reporting technique to be used exclusively on major United States government acquisitions. Earned value is fast becoming a broad-based tool for use on all projects, in all industries. Two recent examples are worthy of discussion because they represent a small sampling of this positive trend.

Located along the Pacific Ocean bluffs, some seventy miles south of Los Angeles, is a major facility of the Southern California Edison Company. It is called the San Onofre Nuclear Generating Station, or SONGS, for short. The SONGS facility, with its two nuclear reactors, provides nearly 20 percent of the electrical power to more than fifteen million residents living in Southern California. The SONGS facility is in effect a little self-contained city of 2,000 employees, with its own information technology (IT) group. It is the IT organization and what it accomplished in 1999 that is worthy of our notice.

Like many IT organizations, the SONGS IT people wanted to know how they compared to other similar groups, using some form of objective measurement. They chose to go the route of the Carnegie Mellon University, with its Software Engineering Institute's (SEI) Capability Maturity Model (CMM) to determine their level of competence. Five levels of SEI CMM competence are achievable, and, as it is with any process improvement, you must take one step at a time. The initial goal of SONGS IT was to take the first step, to attain an SEI CMM level 2 rating by the end of 1999.

The SEI CMM level 2 position is called "repeatable," meaning that basic project management processes are established to track cost, schedule, and functionality. Discipline must be set in place to repeat the successes on similar projects. The management of the SONGS IT organization was aware of the earned value concept and felt that it could be used to effectively manage its software projects. Thus, management purposely set out to incorporate an earned value process into its operating instructions and procedures prior to determining its CMM rating. A series of initiatives were undertaken, including the training of its IT staff. Management deliberately self-imposed an earned value management process on all of its software projects at a threshold of 2,000 hours or more.

(**One Final Note**: The Southern California Edison's SONGS IT organization received its SEI CMM Level 2 rating on 19 December 1999—a job well done, and perhaps an example for other software organizations to follow.)

The Computer Sciences Corporation (CSC) is a major international company with almost 60,000 employees housed in more than 700 offices worldwide. CSC provides a wide array of services to other companies, including IT, electronic-business, outsourcing, consulting, systems integration, and so forth.

Two of the major components of CSC have initiated a series of in-house training courses for their project managers, resulting in the award of a certificate in project management from the University of California at Irvine, their extension division. As an integral goal of this project management training, many of these CSC project managers are sitting for and being awarded the designation of Project Management Professionals (PMP®) from the Project Management Institute.

One of the core courses in this series is entitled Earned Value Project Management. This course and the subject matter are having a positive effect on CSC's project management processes. Many of the CSC project managers are employing their own simplified form of earned value to quickly focus on adverse "hot spots" of performance, allowing them to take corrective measures in time to influence the final results. Another positive example of the employment of earned value by private industry is tailoring the concept to the specific needs of project management.

What do these two examples of earned value project management have in common? Both organizations have found a way to employ earned value on their projects in a simple but effective manner. They have scaled back on the nonvalue-added formal requirements to find the core of the concept. Neither organization would likely pass the rigors of a full and formal government earned-value application, and that is certainly to their credit. They have incorporated what is necessary to employ earned value as an effective project management tool, and have bypassed the other superfluous requirements that would add nothing to their performance. Two truly impressive models that other organizations in private industry could emulate.

Conversion of Earned Value for Broad Use in the Private Sector

It is the belief of the authors that the full and formal application of earned value is appropriate anytime that the risk of cost growth rests with an owner or a governmental body on cost-reimbursable-type contracts. It is only proper in these situations for people to protect their interests by imposing some mechanism to oversee the work being done on their behalf. If the costs go up, then it is the owner or agency that must continue to pay the bill to completion. A full and formal Earned Value Management System (EVMS) consistent with the ANSI/EIA 748 Standard is appropriate for all cost-reimbursable-type work.

However, as we all know, most of the projects in the world are not done on a cost-reimbursable-type arrangement. Most projects typically require firm monetary commitments from the project manager. As a rule, projects consist of some form of hard or fixed amount. They are either firm-fixed-price contractually or done for a specific agreed-to amount. The performing project manager assumes all the risks of any cost increase. Thus, under these conditions, the full and formal requirements of earned value can be relaxed, as long as certain fundamental principles are maintained and earned value is accurately measured.

It is our contention that whenever project managers elect to self-impose the earned value technique to protect their personal financial interests, they do *not* require the full and formal process of an EVMS. A simplified approach that captures the essence of the earned value concept is sufficient.

The authors will outline ten basic steps that are required to implement an effective but simplified form of earned value project management.

1. You must define 100 percent of the project's scope, preferably with use of a Work Breakdown Structure (WBS), which must also include the critical "make-or-buy" choices.

Perhaps the single most critical and challenging requisite to employing earned value is the need to define the total project work scope. This is a difficult task for any project. And yet, if one does not define what constitutes 100 percent of the assumed work, how can one ever measure performance in a definitive way? Without setting a 100 percent reference point, how could anyone ever ascertain that they are 10 percent or 20 percent or 25 percent complete with the job?

Realistically, no project will ever define a new job with absolute precision. But one must make some educated assumptions about a new project in order to quantify and decompose the work with sufficient confidence that the effort can then be planned, scheduled, and estimated with some degree of certainty. Anything less, and management will be committing to a new project by providing essentially a "blank check." Vague scope definition begets scope creep.

How does one define a job when, often, specific details are lacking? There are no absolute answers. But one of the most useful of all tools available to any project manager is the WBS. The WBS is to the project manager what the organization chart is to the executive. A WBS allows the project manager to define a new endeavor by laying out all the assumed work within the framework of the WBS, and then decomposing each element into measurable work packages.

Additionally, once the WBS is assumed to constitute a reasonable representation of the new project, it can then be used to take the next steps in the project planning process, including make-or-buy analysis, risk assessment, scheduling; estimating, and ultimately the authorization of budgets to proceed.

2. You must employ a formal planning and scheduling approach that will provide: a Project Master Schedule (PMS), vertical traceability from the PMS to all subordinate project schedules, and the identification of all horizontal constraints.

Perhaps the single most critical tool required to implement earned value is to have a formal scheduling process in place. The project's scheduling system will portray the approved work scope, with each task carefully placed into a specific time frame for performance. In earned value vernacular, the scheduled work (plus its authorized budget) will constitute the project's "planned value." As performance then takes place on the project, that portion of the planned value that is physically completed (plus its budget) becomes the "earned value." Both the planned value and the resulting earned value emanate from the PMS, and must use the same measurement metrics to both plan and then to measure the performance.

The project's scheduling system is thus critical to the employment of earned value because it is the vehicle that represents the project scope, planned value, and resulting earned value. The PMS is vital to earned value projects, because it reflects the project manager's planned value for everyone to follow.

On larger, more complex projects, a hierarchy of schedules may need to be put into place. Each subordinate schedule must reflect the same requirements as was defined by the PMS. Also on complex projects, there must be some method to isolate the constraints between one task and other tasks. Typically, to accomplish this requirement, some form of critical path methodology will need to be used.

3. You must estimate the necessary resources to complete the entire project, based on an assumed definition of project scope.

Once the work scope has been fully defined and subsequently planned and scheduled, the next requirement for forming an earned value baseline is to estimate the resource requirements for all defined tasks within each of the specified WBS elements. Each defined WBS element must have a resource value estimated to complete all of the specified work.

Remember the rule: Planned value represents two things: the scheduled work, plus the estimated resources. Earned value represents two things: the completed work, plus the same estimated resources. Thus, in order to plan and then measure earned value, one needs to schedule all defined tasks along with the estimated costs necessary to complete the tasks.

4. You must determine the points of management control, referred to as Control Account Plans (CAPS), which integrate the project's scope, schedule, and budgets.

Earned value requires an integrated project baseline, meaning that the defined work scope must relate to both the planned schedule and the authorized budget. The integration takes place within the WBS elements.

Project management must specify its points of management focus, referred to in earned value as CAPs. CAPS are placed at selected WBS elements and can best be thought of as subprojects of the full project. The sum of the CAPS will constitute the total project baseline.

The actual performance measurement takes place within each of the specified CAPs, and total project performance is simply the summation of all the detailed CAPs.

5. You must authorize each CAP, and assign it to a specific function where someone will assume responsibility for its performance: a vice president, director, senior manager, and so on.

Projects are by their very nature "transient" within any firm's permanent organizational structure. Projects are authorized, implemented, performed, and then they go out of existence. Many (perhaps most) of the control account managers of the performance that takes place within the CAPs will not carry the formal title of "manager" within the permanent organizational structure. Rather, many (perhaps most) of these CAP managers are functional employees temporarily assigned, matrixed into the project, by one of the permanent functional organizations.

In order to secure a firm commitment from the functional executives who have both the authority and resources to make the CAP plans actually happen, it is a wise practice to have each of the authorized project CAPs adopted by a senior functional person, who may carry a title such as vice president, director, manager, supervisor, and the like.

6. You must establish a Performance Measurement Baseline (PMB), made up from the sum of the CAPs, which may sometimes include indirect costs, Management Reserves (MR), and even profits.

The next required step is to form a total project baseline against which performance may be measured for the duration of the project. Such baselines must include all the authorized CAPs, plus they sometimes will include management (or contingency) reserves that may be controlled by the project manager. If MR are not allotted to the project manager—rather, they are controlled by a management oversight committee—then they should be excluded from the project performance baseline.

On commercial-type contracts, the project baseline may sometimes include such things as indirect costs, and even profits or fee, to match the total authorized project commitment. The project baseline must include whatever senior management has authorized the project manager to accomplish.

Internal company projects will typically not contain indirect costs, profits, or MR. Many (perhaps most) internal project baselines will simply represent the sum of the defined CAPs, made up exclusively from direct labor hours.

7. You must periodically determine the project's schedule results by comparing the earned value achieved against the PMS, and also determine the cost results by periodically comparing the earned value achieved against the actual costs incurred to accomplish the work.

Projects employing earned value need to monitor their cost and schedule results against the authorized baseline for the duration of the project. Management should focus its attention on exceptions to the baseline plan that are beyond acceptable limits or tolerances.

A negative earned value schedule variance simply means that the value of the work performed does not match the value of the work scheduled; that is, the project is falling behind in its scheduled work plan. Each behind-schedule task should be assessed as to its criticality. If the late task is on the critical path, or if the task carries a high risk to the project, then efforts can be taken to get the late task back on schedule. Additional project resources should not be wasted on low-risk tasks that have positive float.

However, the single most important aspect of employing earned value is the cost efficiency readings that it provides. The difference between the value of work performed versus the costs incurred to accomplish the work provides the cost efficiency factor. If the project spends more money than it receives in value, then this reflects an overrun condition. Absolute overruns are typically nonrecoverable. Overruns expressed as a percentage value have been found to deteriorate ... unless the project takes aggressive actions to mitigate the condition.

Perhaps of greatest benefit, the earned value cost-efficiency rate has been found to be stable from the 15 percent point of a project completion. The cost-efficiency factor is an important metric for any project manager or enterprise executive to monitor.

8. You must periodically forecast the final cost results within a statistical range of values, reflecting the best- and worst-case scenarios.

One of the more beneficial aspects of earned value is that it provides the capability to quickly and independently forecast the total funds required to complete a project, commonly referred to as the estimate at completion. Based on actual cost and schedule performance against its own plan, a project is able to accurately estimate the total funds that it will require to finish the job within a finite range of values. The earned value statistical estimates constitute a sort of "sanity check" against other forecasts or set management positions. Often individuals have a preconceived notion of what final costs should be, or what they would like them to be, and their position is unmovable.

If the earned value statistical range of estimates is greater than the "official" project manager's estimate to complete the project, someone needs to reconcile these professional differences of opinion.

9. You must continuously keep management at all levels apprised of the performance results, allowing it to direct corrective actions in order to stay on the authorized course. Earned value provides one set of books for everyone to watch: executive management, functional management, the customer, and the project manager.

The actual performance results on any project, good or bad, are in effect "sunk costs." Thus, any improvements in performance must come from future work, tasks that lie ahead of the project status date. Earned value allows the project manager to accurately measure the cost and schedule performance achieved to date. And if the results achieved to date are less than that desired by management, then the project can exert a more aggressive posture to manage all future work.

Earned value, because it allows the project to accurately quantify the value of the work that it has achieved, also allows the project to quantify the value of the future work in order to stay within the objectives set for the project by management. Thus, corrective actions can be taken early to stay within the final management expectations.

10. You must manage all changes to the defined project scope, approving or rejecting all change requests and incorporating all approved changes into a new PMB.

The project PMB, which was initially put into place at the start of the project, is only as good as the management of all proposed changes to the baseline for the duration of the project. Performance baselines become invalid simply by failing to incorporate changes into the approved baseline, by the addition or elimination of added work scope.

All new change requests of the project must be carefully addressed, either approving such changes or rejecting them. In order for the initial baseline to remain valid, each and every change must be controlled. Maintaining a baseline is as challenging as the initial definition of the project scope at the start of the project.

In Summary

There is nothing inherent with the earned value concept that precludes it from broad-based applications to all projects, not simply limited to major government acquisitions. However, in its present form as a part of the EVMS, there are just too many nonvalue-added requirements to use it as a universal tool for applications in the private sector. We are advocates of earned value management for the mission for which it was created: to manage the contractual performance of a "stranger to stranger," "government to industry" relationship. The EVMS is an excellent vehicle to monitor and oversee and verify such relationships.

What we are suggesting, however, is that each company and project manager should make his or her own assessment of the utility of earned value and, in effect, "reengineer" the process to best fit one's own particular needs. Companies should certainly move away from the "plan-versus-actual-costs" approach to monitor project's cost performance. Such comparisons are useful only to forecast project-funding requirements. If staying within the project's funding is all that is important to a project, and perhaps that is sometimes the case, then plan-versus-actual-costs metrics may be all that is needed. However, if one wants to understand what one is getting for the money being spent, then earned value project management likely is for you.

What is suggested is that projects move from the plan versus actual costs standard and on to a simple and "scalable" earned value measurement approach. Company management at all levels will then be versed in the use of earned value performance metrics to monitor its projects. It could then easily shift from minimal but effective applications up to a full EVMS covering all projects in its company's portfolio.

Chapter 12

Earned Value Project Management: A Fiduciary Duty

Fiduciary: A person having a duty, created by his undertaking, to act primarily for another's benefit in matters connected with such undertaking. The term is not restricted to technical or express trusts, but also includes such offices or relations as those of an attorney at law, a guardian, executor, or broker, a director of a corporation, and a public officer.

Black's Law Dictionary

Any person who – (2) offers or sells a security ... which includes an untrue statement of a material fact or omits to state a material fact necessary in order to make the statements, in the light of the circumstances under which they were made, not misleading ... shall be liable to the person purchasing such security from him, who may sue either at law or in equity in any court of competent jurisdiction, to recover the consideration paid for such security with interest thereon ...

The Securities Act of 1933

Agency submissions should demonstrate that the asset request is justified ... and will be measured using an earned value management system or similar system.

Office of Management and Budget
Capital Programming Guide 1997

The rules requiring a full and complete disclosure of the true financial condition of any company offering its stock to the public have not changed in the almost seventy years since Congress enacted its landmark Securities

Act of 1933 and its companion Securities Exchange Act of 1934. Companies and their executives, who want the public to buy their stock, must provide all prospective buyers with a truthful description of the financial health of their companies.

Today, class-action lawsuits are still being initiated against companies and their executives by individuals alleging that they purchased publicly traded stocks without receiving an accurate disclosure of the true financial health of these firms. These 1933 and 1934 laws are still being cited as justification for taking such legal actions. The central issues often rest on the true financial condition of the firm's assets, its projects that were started but not finished at the time of public announcements. What did the executives really know and disclose at the time that they sold stock to the public.

However, what may have constituted a full disclosure of the facts in the year 1933 may well be different than what constitutes a complete financial disclosure in this, the start of the twenty-first century. The business environment is different, and we can attribute that fact to at least two significant changes. These changes affect, in particular, those publicly held companies or governmental agencies where the bulk of operations are made up of "projects," one-time only jobs that carry specific goals of technical features, time, and costs. Today, all publicly held companies, public agencies, and their executives in charge may effectively have a higher standard of full disclosure to meet than was the case when these two laws were originally passed many years ago.

First, the ability of all individuals and organizations to communicate with one another has expanded dramatically, most significantly in the last decade. The Internet, email, and other advances in information technology and telecommunications have made it possible for us to communicate anytime from even the most remote parts of the world. One can no longer suggest that he or she was not near a telephone to provide an excuse for not communicating openly and completely.

Second, over the past three decades, a little known but highly effective management technique has been demonstrated to be effective in the management of project assets, to determine their true performance status, and to predict the final cost and schedule results ... early in the life cycle of such projects. This technique is called "earned value" management, and its proven track record for the past three decades has been nothing less than spectacular.

Thus, with exceptional communications available to everyone, including corporate and governmental officials, and a reliable tool available to any project manager to determine the true cost status of each project, the duty of executives to provide the public with an accurate assessment on a company's financial health has reached new levels of responsibility. The duty to tell all, and to tell it accurately, including both the good and the bad, has never been greater on corporate and governmental officials. Some choose to call this responsibility a "fiduciary duty."

Additionally, with the recent passage of a series of Congressional Acts, and the specific requirements contained in the Office of Management and Budget Circular A-11, cited earlier, the duty of government executives to also employ proven management tools, including Earned Value Management (EVM), can no longer be in question.

Management of Organizations by Projects

It is not uncommon to encounter both public and private organizations that are made up essentially of their projects. Their projects will start and end, and the profitability of the firm is determined by how well it has managed each of its individual projects. The term "management by projects" has been coined to describe such organizational environments.

Within such companies, it is particularly challenging to assess the true status of those projects that begin in one fiscal year and do not complete until a subsequent fiscal year. What is the true value of the work in progress, what are the actual costs incurred to achieve the physical progress, what are the forecasted funds needed to fully complete the project, and so forth? These are not insignificant matters for any organization or company made up primarily of their projects.

The central issue to be discussed: Whenever such companies report on their financial conditions, certain individuals within such companies must make an educated estimate of how well or how poorly the firm is performing on all the projects that may have been started, but not yet finished, at the time of their financial reporting. Someone must make an intelligent assessment, based on whatever data he or she feels may be appropriate, of how much money the company will likely earn or lose on each of its projects when those jobs are finally completed. In order to report their financial positions each year, these companies must forecast the final estimated profit and/or loss for each of their ongoing projects.

It is the contention of the authors that individuals who are placed into positions of responsibility by virtue of the offices that they hold must accurately assess and report the true performance of their projects. They must use every reliable technique available to them. As we begin the twenty-first century, such forecasting methods must include the employment of "earned value" management to accurately determine the true cost and schedule status of all projects. Anything less would represent a breach of these individuals' fiduciary duties to accurately report on the true performance status of their projects. Those persons within private corporations who would have this fiduciary duty would include, at a minimum: chief executive officers, chief financial officers, chief information officers, and the various project managers, themselves. Those executives serving within governmental bodies would carry similar titles, which would vary by organization.

Federal Requirements for EVM

The United States (U.S.) federal government currently invests about $70 billion annually in ongoing funding to projects. Outside of the Department of Defense (DOD), which employs earned value quite well on its major acquisition systems, and a few isolated agencies also employing the technique, not much true "performance measurement" has taken place in the past on most federal government projects.

In this nonmeasured environment, spending all of the allotted project funding becomes the prime objective of many agencies. Any funds not spent by year's end become a candidate for other uses. Any unfinished work on this year's project ... simply gets moved into next year's funding. Let us pause and reflect on this environment for a minute.

If a project spends all of its allocated funding but completes only part of the actual targeted work, and then is allowed to move the unfinished work into next year's funding bucket, what would you call this condition? Some might suggest that this condition should be called an "overrun." But who really knows? No one, outside of a few program managers within the DOD, is watching a project's true cost efficiency rate—that is, the relationship between the value of the actual work against the actual costs being incurred or spent.

Many individuals within the Government have been concerned about this very issue: *What are we (the government) getting for what we are spending?* Beginning in 1993, the U.S. Congress has passed three new laws that have required some form of performance measurement on all federally funded projects. These three acts are: Government Performance Results Act of 1993, Federal Acquisition Streamlining Act of 1994, and Information Technology Management Reform Act of 1996.

These laws have since prompted the Office of Management and Budget (OMB) to take action by issuing a new OMB Circular No. A-11 entitled *Planning, Budgeting, and Acquisition of Fixed Assets.* The term "fixed assets" includes most of the projects being funded by the government, *including* information technology projects. Circular A-11 defines a cost variance in a manner that leaves no doubt of its intent to focus on true project earned value cost efficiencies:

> Cost Variance. Earned value compared with the actual cost incurred (from contractor accounting systems) for the work performed provides an objective measure of planned and actual cost. Any difference is called a cost variance (OMB July 1997).

Still another encouraging sign was contained in the documentation requirements to justify the fiscal year 1998 budget submittals. One of the key submittal documents was entitled *Principles of Budgeting for Capital Asset Acquisitions.* In this new federal guide, the phrase "by using earned value management system or similar system" is used in seven distinct places (OMB 1997).

Whether or not there will be earned value performance measurement on the projects being funded by the federal government each year, only time will tell. What is encouraging is that both the executive branch and Congress have taken some positive moves to require earned value measurement on all federally funded projects.

In Summary

In this closing discussion, we have attempted to make the case for employing a concept in the management of projects called earned value. It is our belief that EVM has been proven to be an effective tool, based on documented performance history accumulated on hundreds of actual projects, albeit mostly with the U.S. DOD and predominately on cost-reimbursable-type projects.

But the real opportunities for earned value lie within private industry, on projects where the private firm has made firm fixed-price commitments, where all of the risks of cost growth reside squarely with the performing company. In these environments, there is very limited use of the earned value concept today, and what a pity. In its basic but simplified form, earned value can be a most powerful tool for any project manager.

It has been the contention of the authors that there is often a duty created on the part of selected corporate officers and governmental officials, based on the offices that they hold. That duty would require them to employ all proven management tools in the performance of their jobs, including, and in particular, EVM.

This duty would extend to project managers, the chief financial officers, chief information officers, and certainly the chief executive officers of most corporations. With the recent new laws enacted by Congress, this duty likely also would extend into governmental agencies that have projects to manage within their organizations.

These individuals can in part meet this fiduciary duty by employing a simple but effective form of earned value in the management of their projects.

Appendix I

The Earned Value Management System Criteria

Since the introduction of Earned Value Management (EVM) to industry on 22 December 1967, the United States (U.S.) Department of Defense (DOD) has consistently defined its requirements for its use through a series of management system criteria to be met by any company wishing to do business with the DOD. These criteria were originally specified within the DOD Instruction 7000.2, entitled *Performance Measurement for Selected Acquisitions.*

This formal document imposed thirty-five Cost/Schedule Control Systems Criteria (C/SCSC) on private industry anytime that it wished to acquire a new major system from the DOD. Over the years, other agencies of the U.S. government and many foreign governments (most notably, Australia, Canada, New Zealand, and Sweden) have adapted identical or similar criteria for companies in the private sector to follow.

When the DOD elected to transfer these earned value criteria into its acquisition policy document, DOD Instruction 5000.2R, on 23 February 1991, these same thirty-five criteria remained unchanged. Thus, since their inception and initial release by the DOD in 1967, the thirty-five EVM criteria have remained consistent.

Then on 18 April 1995, at a formal meeting of the Management Systems Subcommittee of the National Defense Industrial Association (NDIA) in Phoenix, Arizona, the NDIA subcommittee took on the task of reexamining and possibly rewriting the DOD's earned value criteria. Its stated objective: to make the criteria more user friendly, more compatible with the needs of private industry. Over the next few months, the NDIA subcommittee met, discussed, and established its own reworded version of the thirty-five C/SCSC. When released, the industry version was now called the Earned Value Management System (EVMS) criteria and contained just thirty-two criteria, three less than the original C/SCSC.

In a somewhat bold move on 14 December 1996, the then Under Secretary of Defense for Acquisition & Technology, Dr. Paul Kaminski, accepted the industry thirty-two EVM criteria verbatim. The industry EVMS criteria were then incorporated into the next update of the DOD Manual 5000.2R in 1997.

The significance of these changes did not lie in the revised wording of the criteria, or in the minimal reduction in their number from thirty-five to thirty-two. Rather, the critical change that took place was in the "attitude" toward the earned value process. During 1997, there was a shifting of the EVMS ownership from that of a U.S. government requirement to that of ownership by private industry. Private industry now embraced the EVM technique, not because it was government mandated, but because it represented a "best practice" tool available to all project managers in the private sector.

One final postscript deserves mention. The NDIA subcommittee continued its work of converting EVM into a broad-based international best practice. The NDIA subcommittee requested that the revised EVM criteria be formally issued as an American National Standards Institute/ Electronic Industries Association (NSIA/EIA) standard. In July 1998, NSIA/EIA Standard 748 was formally released. Then on 17 August 1999, Dr. Jacques S. Gansler, the new Under Secretary of Defense for Acquisition and Technology, accepted the ANSI/EIA 748 standard for applications to all DOD projects, formally superseding the C/SCSC.

What follows is a description of the thirty-two industry EVMS criteria, together with our "unofficial" interpretation of each criterion. These thirty-two criteria are divided into five major groupings. Please understand that the interpretative narrative that follows represents the authors' views, and only their views. Others may look at these same criteria and take different interpretations of their meaning. As we have done on other occasions, we did not wait to obtain a consensus on our position.

Group 1—Organization Criteria (five)

The first group of criteria deals with the requirement for any new project to be completely defined and planned prior to starting performance of the work. Today, we would typically call this effort "defining the scope of the project." Earned value performance cannot be measured without a definition of what constitutes 100 percent of the project.

This effort starts with a requirement to specify all of the assumed project work to be accomplished. It is recommended that such definitions be accomplished with the use of a Work Breakdown Structure (WBS) in order to completely capture all of the proposed work. The WBS provides for the integration of all project tasks, together with their estimated resources, and each task planned within a specific time frame for performance. Once defined, some one individual or organization is held accountable for the performance of each of the defined project tasks.

Any comprehensive definition of project scope must include the make-versus-buy decisions for all segments of work that will be procured from other (outside) organizations. Managers responsible for the authorization and control of indirect costs must also be identified.

The major problems in meeting these initial criteria have been an inadequate definition of the total project scope, a poorly or zero definition of make versus buy, and the rejection of the project manager's WBS by selected but key functional organizations.

EVM Criterion # 1

Define the authorized work elements for the program. A WBS, tailored for effective internal management control, is commonly used in this process.

The first criterion requires that any new project completely define all of the effort before the performance begins. A WBS typically is recommended (required) for use in this process. A WBS is a product-oriented hierarchical family tree that describes the major segments of project effort and is used to specify all deliverables: hardware, software, services, and data. The WBS used to specify all of the assumed work is perhaps the single most important requirement to the employment of earned value. Each WBS level provides a progressively more detailed description of the work to be accomplished.

All contract line items and deliverable products should be specified somewhere within the WBS. All organizational functions must work within the scope defined by the project WBS. Any work that is requested of the project that cannot be identified within the WBS is potentially an out-of-scope effort, and authorization is needed in order to accomplish such work.

The project WBS allows management to focus on a logical grouping of project work for performance measurement. At the lowest selected levels of specified WBS elements will be placed Control Account Plans, or CAPs, which are the points where earned value performance and management control will take place for the project. A CAP can best be thought of as a subproject, a project team, an integrated product team, or perhaps simply as a point of management control.

All CAPs must contain four elements to be viable: an authorized scope of work, a specified time frame for performance, an approved budget, and a person or organization to be held accountable for performance of the CAP. The summation of all specified CAPs will constitute the total project.

EVM Criterion # 2

Identify the program organizational structure, including the major subcontractors responsible for accomplishing the authorized work, and define the organizational elements in which work will be planned and controlled.

This criterion requires that all tasks contained in the project's WBS be identified to a specific internal functional organization for performance, or designated as an external buy item as a part of the project's make-versus-buy process. The project WBS is related to the company Organizational Breakdown Structure (OBS) to assign each of the project's tasks to a specific organization for performance. This process will produce what is called a project tasks-versus-organization responsibility assignment matrix.

All tasks contained in the project WBS must be assigned to a specific organization for performance, even that work that will be procured from outside of the company—that is, contracted or subcontracted to another company for performance. This criterion requires that the project have a specific organization identified to assign all of the defined work tasks.

EVM Criterion # 3

Provide for the integration of the company's planning, scheduling, budgeting, work authorization, and cost accumulation processes with each other, and, as appropriate, the program WBS and the program organizational structure.

The purpose of this criterion is to require the integration of the project's management process with both the way the work was defined with the WBS and the functional organizations performing the effort. This requirement specifies that projects employ a single management control system with a common information database flowing though the contractor's functional disciplines. The CAPs, which have tasks allocated to specific functions, provide the basis for organizations to perform within a common database.

Companies, particularly those with large and well-established functional organizations, often have had difficulty satisfying this criterion. Each of the various functional organizations has its own performance itinerary, and each wants to manage its own affairs in its own particular manner, sometimes at odds with project goals. Not surprising. Master scheduling, cost estimating, work authorizations, budgeting, cost accumulation, each of the various functions, and so on must all work within a single database specified by the project WBS.

The CAP, the fundamental building brick of EVM, made it possible for the various functional units to work from a common database. It allowed contractors to monitor a project from either the WBS, to satisfy the external customer demands, or from the OBS, to satisfy its internal functional customers.

EVM Criterion # 4

Identify the company organization or function responsible for controlling overhead (indirect costs).

U.S. government personnel members associated with the acquisition process were acutely aware, when the criteria were issued, that costs associated with any given project contained both direct and indirect costs. While there is generally minimal controversy over direct project costs, there is much concern over both the content and proportionate application of indirect costs charged to a given project. Thus, four (#s 4, 13, 19, and 24) of the thirty-two criteria deal specifically with the management of indirect costs ... even though any given project manager may have minimal influence over such costs. That is why they are called indirect costs, because they are nonspecific to any given project. Only the very senior executive management can influence indirect costs, not any given project manager.

This criterion requires that all indirect costs as a category be clearly defined and formally documented. Those individual managers who are responsible for authorizing and controlling overheads must be identified, generally with some type of delegation of authority, which stipulates the limits of such authority. These activities may be centralized or decentralized, as long as there is consistency in application and a clear assignment of responsibility.

The allocation of indirect costs to specific projects must be consistent for *all* projects in the organization, and defined somewhere in procedural form. Such costs may not be arbitrarily applied to a given project inconsistent with such procedures. The government is particularly sensitive to the consistency of application of such costs, as they are allotted to different types of contracts within a firm's cost-reimbursable versus fixed-price contracts. Its concern is that contractors might be tempted to maximize profits on their fixed-price work, at the expense of cost-reimbursable (open-ended) efforts.

EVM Criterion # 5

Provide for integration of the program WBS and the program organizational structure in a manner that permits cost and schedule performance measurement by elements of either, or both, structures as needed.

Four (#s 5, 17, 18, and 25) of the thirty-two criteria deal with the issue of putting a baseline in place that can be measured both from the perspective of the project, by WBS, and the functional organization, by the OBS. This is the first of the four criteria dealing with this issue.

This requirement is met by forming CAPs, which can be summarized by either the WBS or the OBS. With the use of multifunctional project team CAPs, the individual work-package tasks within a given CAP must be identified to a specific function in order to satisfy the requirement for an OBS roll-up.

Group 2–Planning, Scheduling, and Budgeting Criteria (ten)

In the second grouping of the criteria, there are ten requirements to satisfy, constituting the largest section. Here it must be demonstrated that the project employs a single, integrated management control system within which it can implement a formal project performance baseline for all defined project scope. Each project must be authorized by management, planned, scheduled, and the resources estimated and then formally budgeted, and all work must be performed within the project's formal baseline.

If the project has set aside any management (or contingency) reserves, such values must be strictly controlled by the project manager (or other senior management) and held outside of the project's performance baseline. All such reserves that are subsequently released by the project manager must be formally transferred into the project's performance baseline. This group requires that a formal management control system be in place for the full life cycle of the project.

There have been several problems experienced with this group of criteria. One of the most common has resulted from a general lack of discipline by the functional organizations supporting the authorized project. It is not possible to measure project performance when the functional departments doing the work are casual or lax about keeping records of their own performance.

Other common problems have been associated with the critical relationship of authorized budget to authorized work tasks contained in the project baseline. The inadvertent (or intentional) front-end placement of budget without a corresponding level of work scope, called "frontloading," and/or the inadvertent (or intentional) shifting of authorized project budget into earlier periods, without a corresponding shifting of work tasks, called "rubber baselining," have created problems for those companies who want to "game" the EVM process.

EVM requires formality and discipline from the full organization performing work on a project, or the measurement of actual performance will be questionable.

EVM Criterion # 6

Schedule the authorized work in a manner that describes the sequence of work and identifies the significant task interdependencies required to meet the requirements of the program.

This criterion requires that contractors have in place a formal scheduling system to support their projects. In particular, the organizations must issue a top Project Master Schedule (PMS) for each project, which sets forth all critical milestones and key tasks for the project. The project's planned value will be determined by compliance with this criterion.

On larger and more complex projects, and in organizations where there are numerous projects being performed simultaneously, PMSs must be reinforced by subordinate schedules, as appropriate, often in the form of detailed functional schedules. However, all schedules within the enterprise must be in concert with the requirements contained in each project's PMS.

The key issue is the traceability and consistency of the key program milestones specified in each PMS. Functions must schedule their work in accordance with the requirements defined in PMSs. The schedules must portray the sequence of all work to be accomplished, and each CAP must contain the baseline start and stop dates, from which project completion dates can be forecasted.

Nowhere in any of the criteria is it specified that a particular scheduling technique must be used. However, the criteria do require that contractor scheduling systems must reflect interdependencies and constraints. Since only Critical Path Method (CPM) schedules show such relationships, a strict interpretation of this criterion might suggest that EVM requires the use of some type of a CPM network schedules.

EVM Criterion # 7

Identify physical products, milestones, technical performance goals, or other indicators that will be used to measure progress.

This criterion is related to #6, and requires that projects have the ability to measure their physical performance, as defined within the tasks displayed in project schedules. What constitutes the physical completion of the work is the central issue.

Projects must specify what physical products, outputs, metrics, milestones, and technical performance indicators will be used to measure work accomplished against the schedule plan. How the earned value actually will be measured is the requirement of this criterion.

There are numerous methods with which to measure physical work accomplishment, and the projects must specify which of these methods they will employ.

EVM Criterion # 8

Establish and maintain a time-phased budget baseline at the control account level, against which program performance can be measured. Initial budgets established for performance measurement will be based on either internal management goals or the external customer-negotiated target cost, including estimates for authorized but undefined work. Budget for far-term efforts may be held in higher-level accounts until an appropriate time for allocation at the control-account level. On government contracts, if an over-target baseline is used for performance measurement reporting purposes, prior notification must be provided to the customer.

When this criterion describes "a time-phased budget baseline," it is imposing a precise term in EVM, the "Performance Measurement Baseline" (PMB). It is important that this term be fully understood. We are discussing the project baseline against which performance will be measured. The PMB is defined in the industry guidelines for EVMS as:

> Performance Measurement Baseline (PMB). The total time-phased budget plan against which program performance is measured. It is the schedule for expenditure of the resources allocated to accomplish program scope and schedule objectives, and is formed by the budgets assigned to control accounts and applicable indirect budgets. The Performance Measurement Baseline also includes budget for future effort assigned to higher Work Breakdown Structure levels (summary level planning packages) plus any undistributed budget. Management Reserve is not included in the baseline as it is not yet designated for specific work scope (National Defense Industrial Association 1996).

The project's PMB is made up of the sum of the project's CAPs. Any Management Reserve (MR) is considered to be outside of the PMB until specifically authorized and allocated for specific work within the PMB.

The PMB must include all authorized project work. Authorized, but not yet defined project work may exist in various forms: authorized but not yet estimated, authorized but not yet proposed, authorized but not yet negotiated, negotiated but not yet covered by a change order, and so on. However, in order to accurately measure performance, all work being done by the project must be included in the PMB.

On projects that run for a long duration, it may be inadvisable or even impossible to budget the far-term effort down to the specific CAP level. In such cases, far-term budgets may be allocated and kept at the higher-level WBS elements in what are called "planning packages." This is simply the "rolling-wave" budgeting technique. It is critical to the integrity of EVMSs that the far-term budgets be tightly controlled to prevent their being co-mingled with the near-term fully budgeted CAPs.

Generally, CAPs should be opened consistent with their scheduled start date, not before. If a situation calls for starting work on a CAP prior to the planned start date, such work must be authorized on an exception basis by the project manager. The across-the-board starting of work earlier than planned could adversely impact authorized funding and distort the performance measurement. The concern is that overruns might be disguised if budgets were allowed to be casually shifted back and forth between time periods.

This criterion also requires that indirect project costs be allocated into the PMB, but not necessarily within the individual CAP budgets. There is no requirement that indirect costs be included within each CAP. However, if left outside of individual CAP budgets, then indirect costs must be allocated in some way so that the full value of the PMB includes both the direct and indirect costs. Some projects accomplish this by creating a separate CAP covering indirect costs.

The term "Over Target Baseline," or OTB as used in the criterion, is a kind, gentle, and ambiguous term for describing an "overrun." For some reason, EVM practitioners, or more likely their management, have always been shy about calling an overrun what it is: an "overrun". The final sentence of this criterion merely suggests that if the project sets its budgets to an OTB or overrun, then it should only do so with the blessing and concurrence of the customer and/or management. We would certainly hope so.

All projects require a well-defined and formally controlled PMB in order to measure earned value performance for the life of the project.

EVM Criterion # 9

Establish budgets for authorized work with identification of significant cost elements (labor, material, and so on.) as needed for internal management and for control of subcontractors.

The total project must be budgeted, and such budgets reflect the type of costs associated with the budgets. Costs that must be identified would be direct labor; the indirect burdens; the various types of procured items, including materials, contracts, or subcontracts; and all other direct costs, such as travel, computer, and so on. Such budgets must be formally controlled according to internal company procedures. The functional organizations receiving the budgets must be identified.

Budgeted values must represent the project costs that have been negotiated. If there have been authorized changes that have not yet been negotiated, then the budgets must include an estimated value for all such authorized work. Contractor budgets must be issued in a formal, documented, and controlled manner down to the CAP level.

EVM Criterion # 10

To the extent that it is practical to identify the authorized work in discrete work packages, establish budgets for this work in terms of dollars, hours, or other measurable units. Where the entire control account is not subdivided into work packages, identify the far-term effort in larger planning packages for budget and scheduling purposes.

Many criteria are related to other criteria, and often will expand on the requirements imposed in other criteria. This one further expands the requirements for a definitive PMB. Here discrete work packages must be created for near-term tasks to the greatest extent possible, followed by larger planning packages in the far term. All budgets must be time-phased over the full life of the project.

Under this criterion, the project must demonstrate that it has established discrete budgets to the greatest extent possible in a way that represents how the work will be performed. All effort that is shown in far-term, time-phased planning packages will subsequently become definitive work packages as it approaches the near-term periods for performance. These criteria previously have specified that discrete work packages must be of relatively short duration, but that wording was dropped in the revision to the criteria.

All work packages must contain measurable metrics to allow for the calculation of work measurement. The project must be able to differentiate between near-term work packages and far-term planning packages, so that specified work and budget cannot be indiscriminately shifted.

All direct budgets must be expressed in measurable units—for example, dollars, hours, standards, or other types of measurable costs. All work-package tasks must be assigned to a specific function for performance.

EVM Criterion # 11

Provide that the sum of all work-package budgets, plus planning-package budgets within a control account, equals the control-account budget.

This criterion simply requires that the sum of all work-package budgets and planning-package budgets within any CAP must equal the authorized budget for the CAP. All authorized budgets must relate to a specific Statement of Work (SOW) to be performed, except for management reserve budgets that are held outside of the performance baseline.

EVM Criterion # 12

Identify and control level-of-effort activity by time-phased budgets established for this purpose. Only that effort that is unmeasurable, or for which measurement is impractical, may be classified as level of effort.

This criterion allows for EVM by use of Level Of Effort (LOE), but only for that work that cannot be measured with either discrete or apportioned means. Of the three types of work tasks to be measured with earned value (discrete, apportioned, or LOE), without question LOE measurement is the least desirable.

LOE tasks must be identified, time phased, and kept to a minimum. With LOE tasks, the earned value accomplished always equals the planned value, irrespective of whether any work was done at all. LOE, in effect, measures the passage of time, not physical work accomplishment.

This criterion requires that LOE budgets, when used, must be formally budgeted and controlled as with any other effort. Neither budget nor earned value for the LOE tasks may be shifted independently to the left or right, for this would distort the reported status of a project.

Examples of typical LOE efforts are the project manager and staff, a field support engineer, guard services, scheduling, help information desks, and so on, each of which performs activities more related to time passage than to output. Certain tasks may be justifiable as LOE, but they must be kept to a minimum to prevent the distortion of performance being measured.

EVM Criterion # 13

Establish overhead budgets for each significant organizational component of the company for expenses that will become indirect costs. Reflect in the program budgets, at the appropriate level, the amounts in overhead pools that are planned to be allocated to the program as indirect costs.

Most industrial firms have indirect-type expenses that are allocated over the direct costs. Some of the larger firms may have several categories or pools of indirect costs. Typical categories of such pools might be: engineering burden, manufacturing burden, material burden, general and administrative expenses, and sometimes even a special study or partial field burdens.

Each company must specify the number of indirect pools that it will have, and the types of costs and methods for controlling each of these independent burden centers. Such costs must be tightly managed with each of the respective pools to preclude the possibility of manipulating such costs by a contractor. Any changes to either the direct bases or burden pools must be accommodated according to formal internal procedures.

Lastly, in the event that burdens are not applied to individual control accounts and the criteria do not require application of burdens to CAP budgets, the contractor must indicate at what point in the WBS and organizational summaries these burden costs will be added.

EVM Criterion # 14

Identify management reserves and undistributed budget.

This criterion deals with two categories of project costs: Management Reserves (MB) and Undistributed Budget (UB).

MR, sometimes also called contingency funds, represents an amount of the total budget baseline that is withheld by the project manager to cover the unknowns, the bad things that are sure to happen but cannot be specified with certainty. MR funds are held outside of the project's PMB.

All MR must be tightly controlled, and every transaction that either adds to or takes from the MR must be documented and approved by the project manager. MR are, by definition, outside of the PMB; therefore, no management reserve may be included in either control account budgets or organizational budgets. MR are expected to be consumed during the performance of the project, and, if unconsumed at the conclusion of the project, then MR become underrun.

UB represents funds applicable to project work that has not yet been identified into a specific WBS element. UB is by definition a part of the project's PMB, as contrasted with MR, which are outside of the PMB, until a management decision is made to transfer some portion of them into the PMB.

UB must be allotted against specific SOW and must be time phased and tightly controlled so as to not be used for other work that could mask an overrun. Typically, there are three situations in which undistributed budget may be used:

1. For project changes that are authorized but not negotiated, where interim budgets are kept at a higher WBS level until negotiations are concluded.
2. For negotiated changes that have not yet been budgeted into CAPs.
3. For far-term tasks where it might be pointless to define budgets down to the detailed control account level at the present time (rolling-wave budgeting concept).

EVM Criterion # 15

Provide that the program target cost goal is reconciled with the sum of all internal program budgets and management reserves.

This criterion has its focus on the ability to account for all project funds. Likely, it is a carryover from the time when large cost-reimbursable-type contracts were commonplace and certain unscrupulous contractors would actually overbudget the total funds on a contract, thus assuring an overrun of the project. Today, with electronic spreadsheets available to us, the utility of this criterion is debatable.

Contractors must demonstrate that they have not exceeded the total project costs with their approved budgets, but also have such control processes documented with internal company procedures.

Group 3—Accounting Criteria (six)

In this third grouping of criteria, the emphasis is on the recording of project costs. It requires the segregation of all legitimate direct costs for a given project together with the appropriate application of indirect costs allocated to the project.

All firms doing business in the public sector will have some type of a formal accounting system in place that will utilize generally acceptable standards of accounting. Such records must be available for subsequent audit, if necessary.

However, earned value performance measurement also demands a somewhat unique accounting requirement. EVM projects must be able to record their direct costs at the point where performance measurement is taking place, typically within the CAPs. Such direct costs must be capable of being summarized both through the project's WBS as well as the company functional organization.

Earned value also requires that a PMB plan be created, which permits the project to relate its planned value against earned value to measure its schedule performance, and its earned value against the actual costs to measure its cost performance.

The major difficulty in meeting this group of criteria has been with the synchronization of the planned value, earned value, and actual or accrued costs for the work performed. Also, accounting for purchased materials and contracted or subcontracted work to other companies has been a constant challenge, particularly when progress payments are allowed. Measuring the planned value against the earned value and actual costs for purchased items has represented the ultimate challenge for projects.

EVM Criterion # 16

Record direct costs in a manner consistent with the budgets in a formal system controlled by the general books of account.

This criterion requires the use of acceptable methods of accounting for all direct project costs. Any conventional method of accounting may be used, but the preferred technique is the "applied direct cost" method, which simply means that direct resources are accounted for as used or as consumed. It is fairly easy to allocate direct labor and the corresponding burdens and other direct costs to a specific project. However, direct costs for materials—because they are often purchased for inventory, consumed in a later time period, or may be transferred out of an inventory to another project—often provide a challenge for measuring on any given project.

Also, some contractors, because they have been functionally oriented for so long a time, have difficulty isolating their direct costs against their specific projects.

The next two criteria are related and will be covered together.

EVM Criterion # 17

When a WBS is used, summarize direct costs from control accounts into the WBS without allocation of a single control account to two or more WBS elements.

EVM Criterion # 18

Summarize direct costs from the control accounts into the contractor's organizational elements without allocation of a single control account to two or more organizational elements.

Criteria #s 17 and 18 are related; the only difference between them is the direction of the summation of the detailed control accounts. Number 17 requires the ability to sum control accounts upward into a WBS segregation to reach the total project. Criterion #18 requires the summation of control accounts by the functional organization to higher organizational levels—for example, engineering, manufacturing, quality, purchasing, testing, and so on, to also match the total project costs.

Both criteria prohibit the allocation of a single control account to more than one WBS element or more than one functional organizational unit. Problem: With the increased use of multifunctional project team control accounts, how do you satisfy criterion #18 without an allocation of costs within a single CAP? Answer: You identify specific work packages within the CAP to a specific organization; thus, the allocation of each work package is directly linked to a specific organizational unit.

EVM Criterion # 19

Record all indirect costs that will be allocated to the contract.

Again, here is another criterion that addresses the issue of controlling indirect costs. This requirement is that the contractor be able to sum indirect costs from the point where they are incurred, allocated to specified pools if multiple pools are used, and charged upward to contract totals, and that actual overhead costs be related to the original planned budgets. To satisfy this criterion, there must be a formal documented relationship between those persons who have responsibility for control of indirect budgets and those persons who are able to incur costs against such budgets.

Here the contractor must demonstrate that no manipulation of costs can take place in the allocation of such indirect costs between projects, and that both the commercial work and government contracts are treated properly in the allotment of burden costs.

Lastly, the contractors must be in a position to show that the methods that it uses to allocate indirect costs to the final source are reasonable. Whether the chosen indirect application method calls for a monthly adjustment of indirect actuals against a yearly plan or a constant rate applied and adjusted at year's end for actuals, the procedures governing such activity must be formally documented, in place, and fully auditable.

EVM Criterion # 20

Identify unit costs, equivalent unit costs, or lot costs when needed.

The life cycle for any new product generally consists of two distinct phases: one phase for the product development, and another to manufacture the item over and over again. The developmental phase is considered to be nonrecurring, and the production effort is considered recurring. However, even in the development of a new product, there will often be initial recurring costs involved, and it is a good practice to isolate the nonrecurring from the recurring costs in order to be in a position to later estimate the repetitive costs for producing the new product. Under this criterion, the project must be able to distinguish between nonrecurring (developmental) effort and the recurring (production) effort.

This criterion also requires that the project be able to establish unit, equivalent unit, or lot costs for articles to be subsequently produced in the recurring phase. Unit costs may be developed by direct hours, direct labor dollars, material dollars, or total unit price.

Unit costs may be established by isolating the individual costs of one unit, or by equivalents of units, or by lot costs. Under lot costs, a block of selected units will be produced in a single batch at one time. The contractor must fix the actual average cost of one unit in a given block to satisfy this criterion. The average cost of units in block 1 are then equated to the average unit costs in subsequent blocks 10, 100, 1,000, and so on to determine whether the costs per unit are being reduced, the efficiency increasing, as the articles being manufactured increase.

EVM Criterion # 21

For EVMS, the material accounting system will provide for:
1. *Accurate cost accumulation and assignment of costs to control accounts in a manner consistent with the budgets using recognized, acceptable, costing techniques.*
2. *Cost performance measurement at the point in time most suitable for the category of material involved, but no earlier than the time of progress payments or actual receipt of material*
3. *Full accountability of all material purchased for the program including the residual inventory.*

Without question, this criterion has been the most difficult for contractors to fully satisfy. Certain contractors have actually lost the government's "approval" of their management control systems because they failed to satisfy the demands of this criterion.

The requirement is that all purchased materials be measured in the same accounting period, reflecting their planned value versus the earned value (to reflect the Schedule Variance), and the earned value versus the actual costs (to reflect a Cost Variance). The problem with materials is that these things do not normally happen at the same point in time.

In order to buy something from another company, that something must be defined; that is, a procurement specification must be prepared. But a strict interpretation of item 2 in this criterion precludes giving credit for work in the preparation of a procurement specification, and yet procurements cannot happen without specifications.

Another problem is that, when giving progress payments to suppliers, it is common practice to have "withholds" or "retention" values withheld from the supplier until the entire job has been completed. Thus, there will often be a discrepancy between the earned value compared to the actual costs, unless an accounting accrual is made for the withheld values, which is an added task on the CAP manager.

Last, it is often common practice for one project (the largest) to buy materials for other projects, and place such items into an inventory until used. Item 3 requires a full accountability for all the inventory; not unreasonable, but nevertheless a difficult task to meet.

One recommendation to all projects is to keep purchased material versus in-house labor effort in separate CAPs, because the two do not mix well. Materials must be monitored, and sometimes the actual costs adjusted, by the CAP manager in order to reflect an accurate portrayal of the performance of materials.

Group 4—Analysis Criteria (six)

This fourth grouping of the criteria placed two distinct requirements on projects employing earned value. Both are critical to the proper employment of EVM.

First, the actual performance against the project baseline plan must be monitored, objectively measured, and accurately reported to management. All significant variances from the project baseline plan must be analyzed and understood, and corrective actions taken by management.

Second, based on the actual performance of the project against its own plan, the final required costs and time estimates to complete the project must be routinely forecasted. Such forecasts must be done in time for the project manager to be able to take corrective measures, and thus alter the adverse final projections.

The difficulties typically experienced with this group often included a "subjective" measurement of performance, allowing for a "positive spin" to be put on adverse actual results to artificially improve the progress being reported. Also, projects that allowed an excessive use of LOE tasks to be incorporated into their baseline often had distorted measurements, when their actual staffing fell short of their planned staffing and the positive LOE results masked real problems being experienced that needed attention.

Lastly, senior executive management has often put an unduly optimistic influence on both the reported performance and the forecasts of final costs needed at completion. It wasn't that senior management was trying to deceive anyone; rather they were simply decreeing: "Make the overrun go away!" Sometimes it did, but often it did not.

EVM Criterion # 22

At least on a monthly basis, generate the following information at the control account and other levels, as necessary for management control, using actual cost data from, or reconcilable with, the accounting system:

1. *Comparison of the amount of planned budget and the amount of budget earned for work accomplished. This comparison provides the schedule variance.*
2. *Comparison of the amount of the budget earned and the actual (applied where appropriate) direct costs for the same work. This comparison provides the cost variance.*

This criterion clearly separates EVM from the traditional approach of measuring cost performance by simply relating the planned costs to the actual costs. Here the requirement is for a monthly (at a minimum) comparison of performance at the control account level with a focus on earned value results:

1. Compare the earned value less the planned value, to determine the Schedule Variance (SV).
2. Compare the earned value less the actual costs, to determine the CV.

While this criterion only requires a monthly analysis, the recent experiences in industry would suggest a trend toward the weekly measurement of direct labor hour performance. The comparison should be sufficiently detailed to allow for performance measurement by category of direct costs, subcontractor performance, and organization.

Internal procedures must be in place to require such measurements. If other than actual costs from the general ledger are used to relate cost performance, then there must be a reconciliation with the estimated costs methodology. Lastly, potential overruns or underruns should be predictable from compliance with this criterion.

EVM Criterion # 23

Identify, at least monthly, the significant differences between both planned and actual schedule performance and planned and actual cost performance, and provide the reasons for the variances in the detail needed by program management.

Previously, this criterion only addressed SVs, but with the recent re-wording of the criteria, variances in cost performance was added.

Whenever either an SV or a CV exceeds a previously established acceptable parameter, called a variance threshold, the project must perform an analysis to determine why the acceptable tolerances were exceeded. The analysis should assess the types of costs involved—for example, labor, material, and other direct costs—and discuss the reasons causing such variances. Typically, a plan for recovery should be developed and the future impact on both the final project's cost and schedule determined.

When the project has major segments of its effort performed by another outside company, contracted or subcontracted, and when the supplier's performance exceeds acceptable parameters, the same analysis of results must be performed on the procured effort.

EVM Criterion # 24

Identify budgeted and applied (or actual) indirect costs at the level and frequency needed by management for effective control, along with the reasons for any significant variances.

This criterion requires that a contractor perform an analysis of any variances of indirect expenses against the original budget. The analysis must cover the types of costs involved, and the indirect pool or pools involved, as may be appropriate.

Indirect expenses are applied as a percentage value against a direct cost base. Actual rates may vary from what is originally planned for two principal reasons, because:

1. Indirect expenses actually incurred will vary upward or downward from the original budgeted amounts.
2. The direct business base over which the indirect costs are allocated changes upward or downward, and the indirect costs being applied did not change in a corresponding manner, resulting in a higher or lower allocation to a given project.

The changes that are of primary concern to project management are *increased* indirect expenses over those originally planned, or a *smaller* direct base over which to absorb such costs. In either case, the result will be increased indirect costs applied against a given project. This criterion also requires that some management action be taken in response to adverse changes in the indirect rates.

EVM Criterion # 25

Summarize the data elements and associated variances through the program organization and/or WBS to support management needs and any customer reporting specified in the contract.

Projects are typically required to analyze all significant variances at the control account level. However, projects may not be required to formally report all variances to the customer. Rather, formal customer reporting usually takes place at a higher level of the WBS and at a higher organizational unit.

This approach gives the project some flexibility in managing its effort. Many variances that occur at the control account level are never actually reported to the customer, simply because there are offsetting variances at the same levels of the WBS or OBS. Through corrective actions, projects are often able to bring variances back to acceptable levels without involvement by the customer. There is nothing inherently wrong with this concept, and it gives project managers the opportunity to manage their work without undue customer involvement.

This criterion requires that a project have the ability to summarize variances upward through the WBS, or horizontally by organization unit. Also, there must be consistency in variances being reported to the customer versus that reported internally to management. One set of books only on any project.

EVM Criterion # 26

Implement managerial actions taken as the result of earned value information.

This criterion addresses the issue of whether earned value performance data is being used by management throughout the organization. It requires that there be a procedure in effect that initiates corrective actions whenever established cost or schedule performance parameters have been penetrated.

Variance thresholds may be set at a number of monitoring points, reflecting either plus or minus values. Many projects will set a combination of variance points that trigger some type of management action. Variances, either over or under a given threshold can indicate either a performance problem or sometimes a problem with the authorized baseline plan. Positive variances are often set at a greater value than negative variances, often twice the value, simply because they typically represent a questionable plan, not just poor performance.

EVM Criterion # 27

Develop revised estimates of cost at completion based on performance to date, commitment values for material, and estimates of future conditions. Compare this information with the PMB to identify variances at completion important to company management and any applicable customer-reporting requirements, including statements of funding requirements.

A key issue for all projects is how much it will cost to complete the total project, typically referred to as the estimate at completion, or EAC. Likely, this is precisely why many projects elect to employ EVM: to get a timely and accurate forecast of the total funds needed to complete the project. If it is going to cost more than management has authorized to complete a given job, management deserves to know it as early as possible. Management may elect to not complete a given project and use the remaining funds elsewhere.

Some project managers have been known to put a positive spin on their actual performance results, and perhaps mislead management into unrealistic expectations of the final bill. At other times, it may be senior management who will insist on ignoring the actual performance results and direct the project manager to make overruns "go away." Call it being optimistic, unrealistic, misrepresenting the facts, or whatever; some firms have established a reputation for themselves of consistently making poor projections of the total funding requirements. This is often the case when they are working under cost-reimbursable contracts. Therefore, an essential ingredient in any management control system must be the ability to make accurate and timely forecasts of the final costs on jobs.

This criterion requires that EACs be performed routinely, based on actual performance to date and a reasonable assessment of the work to complete all unfinished contract tasks. Such estimates must relate to the current authorized SOW, and are best supported by bottoms-up estimates of the remaining tasks.

Because of their magnitude on the total costs, overhead or indirect costs are an essential part of any accurate EAC, even though indirect costs will be beyond the control of any given project manager. Historical performance of indirect pools should be considered while forecasting the EAC. Many of the overhead cost items are essentially fixed assets, an administration building, and such costs will not change even though there may be a major drop of direct bases.

A number of issues pertain to the EAC preparations that can be handled best through documented internal procedures. For example, the frequency with which EACs must be prepared is an issue best determined with documented procedures.

Group 5—Revisions Criteria (five)

This last of the five groups of criteria deals with handling revisions to the approved project baseline. All changes to the approved baseline must be aggressively managed, and either approved or rejected in a timely fashion. The quickest way to lose the ability to measure project performance is to ignore changes and work to an obsolete baseline. All such changes to the original baseline must be documented and be traceable back to the original approved baseline.

Changes to a baseline often result from two primary sources: external customer direction or internal management ideas. No project of any magnitude ever runs its full course without encountering some change, and it is incumbent upon a project manager to dispose of all changes in an orderly and documented manner.

Difficulties often arise in the management and incorporation of project changes. Often new work is performed without proper authorization, and subsequent approval never happens. Sometimes the change approval process is slow, never catching up the performance baseline.

EVM Criterion # 28

Incorporate authorized changes in a timely manner, recording the effects of such changes in budgets and schedules. In the directed effort prior to negotiation of a change, base such revisions on the amount estimated and budgeted to the program organizations.

All projects encounter changes both from external and internal sources. In order to maintain a relationship between the work authorized and the actual physical work being performed, a project must incorporate changes into approved budgets in a timely manner.

Just what constitutes "timely" is a debatable question. In some cases, "timely" could represent minutes, as when stopping work for a safety issue. In other situations, it might allow for days or weeks to pass before incorporation. The outer limit of "timely" likely would be dictated by the project's reporting cycle to management. There must be consistency on what is being reported and what is being actually worked.

Changes to the working budgets and schedules must be accommodated in an expeditious manner and reflected in the project's baseline. Work that has been authorized but not negotiated with the customer must be folded into the baseline, based on an estimated value of the new work, and, once negotiated, adjusted to reflect the final settlement with the customer. Newly authorized but unpriced work must be planned and controlled, as with all defined work.

EVM Criterion # 29

Reconcile current budgets to prior budgets, in terms of changes to the authorized work and internal replanning in the detail needed by management for effective control.

This criterion requires traceability of all changes currently being worked back to the original project baseline. Since earned value baselines are constructed from bottoms-up detail, this requirement is satisfied by providing traceability down to the lowest level of the project WBS.

EVM Criterion # 30

Control retroactive changes to records pertaining to work performed that would change previously reported amounts for actual costs, earned value, or budgets. Adjustments should be made only for correction of errors, routine accounting adjustments, effects of customer- or management-directed changes, or to improve the baseline integrity and accuracy of performance measurement data.

EVM requires discipline from the organization. Measurement of project performance must be objective to the greatest extent possible. If "after-the-fact" changes to the planned value, earned value, or actual costs can be made, then the temptation to manipulate the report card will exist. This criterion prevents the indiscriminate altering of past period data without a documented justification, and includes both direct and indirect costs.

An exception to this rule may be allowed to correct errors in calculations and correction of legitimate routine accounting adjustments. In each case, such adjustments should be documented by the person making such changes.

EVM Criterion # 31

Prevent revisions to the program budget, except for authorized changes.

A project baseline will be comprised of that which has been authorized in formal budgets, plus any MR held by the project manager. MR are expected to be consumed during the course of project performance.

Sometimes a project will experience difficulties in staying within the total limits of its authorized budget and, after careful analysis of the work remaining, determines that it would make no sense to continue to measure progress against unattainable cost goals. When such conditions occur, this criterion permits the contractor to budget the work greater than the project baseline, but only with strict approval of senior management or a customer on cost-reimbursable contracts.

The project must have procedures that prevent proceeding with any baseline until approval is received from senior management.

EVM Criterion # 32

Document changes to the PMB.

Maintenance of the approved project baseline is fundamental to EVM. This criterion requires that the project have in place the necessary procedures to preclude unauthorized changes to the project baseline, and that all such changes be traceable back to the original baseline.

Appendix II

A Comparison of the Original Thirty-Five C/SCSC with the Industry Thirty-Two EVMS Criteria

DOD Cost/Schedule Control Systems Criteria (C/SCSC) (35)	INDUSTRY Earned Value Management System (EVMS) (32)
ORGANIZATION: 5	ORGANIZATION: 5
1. Define all authorized work and related resources to meet the requirements of the contract, using the framework of the CWBS.	1. Define the authorized work elements for the program. A Work Breakdown Structure (WBS), tailored for effective internal management control, is commonly used in this process.
2. Identify the internal organizational elements and the major subcontractors responsible for accomplishing the authorized work.	2. Identify the program organizational structure, including the major subcontractors responsible for accomplishing the authorized work, and define the organizational elements in which work will be planned and controlled.
3. Provide for the integration of the contractor's planning, scheduling, budgeting, work authorization and cost accumulation systems with each other, the CWBS, and the organizational structure.	3. Provide for the integration of the company's planning, scheduling, budgeting, work authorization, and cost accumulation processes with each other, and, as appropriate, the program WBS and the program organizational structure.
4. Identify the managerial positions responsible for controlling overhead (indirect costs).	4. Identify the company organization or function responsible for controlling overhead (indirect costs).
5. Provide for integration of the CWBS with the contractor's functional organizational structure in a manner that permits cost and schedule performance measurement for CWBS and organizational elements.	5. Provide for integration of the program WBS and the program organizational structure in a manner that permits cost and schedule performance measurement by elements of either or both structures as needed.

DOD Cost/Schedule Control Systems Criteria (C/SCSC) (35)	INDUSTRY Earned Value Management System (EVMS) (32)
PLANNING and BUDGETING: 11	PLANNING, SCHEDULING and BUDGETING: 10
1. Schedule the authorized work in a manner that describes the sequence of work and identifies the significant task interdependencies required to meet the development, production, and delivery requirements of the contract.	6. Schedule the authorized work in a manner that describes the sequence of work and identifies significant task interdependencies required to meet the requirements of the program.
2. Identify physical products, milestones, technical performance goals, or other indicators that will be used to measure output.	7. Identify physical products, milestones, technical performance goals, or other indicators that will be used to measure progress.
3. Establish and maintain a time-phased budget baseline at the cost account level against which contract performance can be measured. Initial budgets established for this purpose will be based on the negotiated target cost. Any other amount used for performance measurement purposes must be formally recognized by both the contractor and the government.	8. Establish and maintain a time-phased budget baseline, at the control account level, against which program performance can be measured. Initial budgets established for performance measurement will be based on either internal management goals or the external customer-negotiated target cost, including estimates for authorized but undefinitized work. Budgets for far-term efforts may be held in higher-level accounts until an appropriate time for allocation at the control account level. On government contracts, if an over-target baseline is used for performance measurement reporting purposes, prior notification must be provided to the customer.
4. Establish budgets for all authorized work with separate identification of cost elements (labor, material, and so on.).	9. Establish budgets for authorized work with identification of significant cost elements (labor, material, and so on) as needed for internal management and for control of subcontractors.
5. To the extent the authorized work can be identified in discrete, short-span work packages, establish budgets for this work in terms of dollars, hours, or other measurable units. Where the entire cost account cannot be subdivided into detailed work packages, identify far-term effort in larger planning packages for budget and scheduling purposes.	10. To the extent it is practical to identify the authorized work in discrete work packages, establish budgets for this work in terms of dollars, hours, or other measurable units. Where the entire control account is not subdivided into work packages, identify the far-term effort in larger planning packages for budget and scheduling purposes.
6. Provide that the sum of all work package budgets, plus planning package budgets, within a cost account equals the cost account budget.	11. Provide that the sum of all work package budgets plus planning package budgets within a control account equals the control account budget.
7. Identify relationships of budgets or standards in work authorization systems to budgets for work packages.	This criterion was cancelled.

DOD Cost/Schedule Control Systems Criteria (C/SCSC) (35)	INDUSTRY Earned Value Management System (EVMS) (32)
PLANNING and BUDGETING: 11	**PLANNING, SCHEDULING and BUDGETING: 10**
8. Identify and control level-of-effort activity by time-phased budgets established for this purpose. Only that effort that cannot be identified as discrete, short-span work packages or as apportioned effort may be classed as level of effort.	12. Identify and control level-of-effort activity by time-phased budgets established for this purpose. Only that effort that is unmeasurable or for which measurement is impractical may be classified as level of effort.
9. Establish overhead budgets for the total costs of each significant organizational component whose expenses will become indirect costs. Reflect in the contract budgets at the appropriate level the amounts in overhead pools that are planned to be allocated to the contract as indirect costs.	13. Establish overhead budgets for each significant organizational component of the company for expenses that will become indirect costs. Reflect in the program budgets, at the appropriate level, the amounts in overhead pools that are planned to be allocated to the program as indirect costs.
10. Identify management reserves and undistributed budget.	14. Identify management reserves and undistributed budget.
11. Provide that the contract target cost plus the estimated cost of authorized but unpriced work is reconciled with the sum of all internal contract budgets and management reserves.	15. Provide that the program target cost goal is reconciled with the sum of all internal program budgets and management reserves.

DOD Cost/Schedule Control Systems Criteria (C/SCSC) (35)	INDUSTRY Earned Value Management System (EVMS) (32)
ACCOUNTING: 7	ACCOUNTING CONSIDERATIONS: 6
1. Record direct costs on an applied or other acceptable basis in a manner consistent with the budgets in a formal system that is controlled by the general books of account.	16. Record direct costs in a manner consistent with the budgets in a formal system controlled by the general books of account.
2. Summarize direct costs from cost accounts into the work breakdown structure without allocation of a single cost account to two or more work breakdown structure elements.	17. When a work breakdown structure is used, summarize direct costs from control accounts into the work breakdown structure without allocation of a single control account to two or more work breakdown structure elements.
3. Summarize direct costs from the cost accounts into the contractor's functional organizational elements without allocation of a single cost account to two or more organizational elements.	18. Summarize direct costs from the control accounts into the contractor's organizational elements without allocation of a single control account to two or more organizational elements.
4. Record all indirect costs which will be allocated to the contract.	19. Record all indirect costs which will be allocated to the contract.
5. Identify the bases for allocating the cost of apportioned effort.	**This Criterion was cancelled.**
6. Identify unit costs, equivalent unit costs, or lot costs as applicable.	20. Identify unit costs, equivalent units costs, or lot costs when needed.
7. The contractor's material accounting system will provide for: (1) Accurate cost accumulation and assignment of costs to cost accounts in a manner consistent with the budgets using recognized, acceptable costing techniques. (2) <u>Determination of price variances by comparing planned versus actual commitments.</u> (3) Cost performance measurement at the point in time most suitable for the category of material involved, but no earlier than the time of actual receipt of material. (4) <u>Determination of cost variances attributable to the excess usage of material.</u> (5) <u>Determination of unit or lot costs when applicable.</u> (6) Full accountability for all material purchased for the contract, including the residual inventory.	21. For EVMS, the material accounting system will provide for: (1) Accurate cost accumulation and assignment of costs to control accounts in a manner consistent with the budgets using recognized, acceptable, costing techniques. (2) Cost performance measurement at the point in time most suitable for the category of material involved, but no earlier than the time of progress payments or actual receipt of material. (3) Full accountability of all material purchased for the program including the residual inventory.

DOD Cost/Schedule Control Systems Criteria (C/SCSC) (35)	INDUSTRY Earned Value Management System (EVMS) (32)
ANALYSIS: 6	**ANALYSIS & MGMT. REPORTS: 6**
1. Identify at the cost account level on a monthly basis using data from, or reconcilable with, the accounting system: (1) Comparison of budgeted cost for work scheduled and budgeted cost of work performed; (2) Comparison of budgeted cost for work performed and actual (applied where appropriate) direct costs for the same work; and (3) Variances resulting from the comparisons between the budgeted cost for work scheduled and the budgeted cost for work performed and between the budgeted cost for work performed and actual or applied direct costs, classified in terms of labor, material, or other appropriate elements together with the reasons for significant variances.	22. At least on a monthly basis, generate the following information at the control account and other levels as necessary for management control using actual cost data from, or reconcilable with, the accounting system: (1) Comparison of the amount of planned budget and the amount of budget earned for work accomplished. This comparison provides the schedule variance. (2) Comparison of the amount of the budget earned the actual (applied where appropriate) direct costs for the same work. This comparison provides the cost variance.
4. Identify significant differences on a monthly basis between planned and actual schedule accomplishment and the reasons.	23. Identify, at least monthly, the significant differences between both planned and actual schedule performance and planned and actual cost performance, and provide the reasons for the variances in the detail needed by program management.
2. Identify on a monthly basis, in the detail needed by management for effective control, budgeted indirect costs, actual indirect costs, and cost variances with the reasons for significant variances.	24. Identify budgeted and applied (or actual) indirect costs at the level and frequency needed by management for effective control, along with the reasons for any significant variances.
3. Summarize the data elements and associated variances listed in subparagraphs a.(1) and (2), directly above, through the contractor organization and work breakdown structure to the reporting level specified in the contract.	25. Summarize the data elements and associated variances through the program organization and/or work breakdown structure to support management needs and any customer reporting specified in the contract.
5. Identify managerial actions taken as a result of criteria items 1. through 4. above.	26. Implement managerial actions taken as the result of earned value information.
6. Based on performance to date, on commitment values for material, and on estimates of future conditions, develop revised estimates of cost at completion for work breakdown structure elements identified in the contract and compare these with the contract budget base and the latest statement of funds requirements reported to the Government.	27. Develop revised estimates of cost at completion based on performance to date, commitment values for material, and estimates of future conditions. Compare this information with the performance measurement baseline to identify variances at completion important to company management and any applicable customer reporting requirements including statements of funding requirements.

DOD Cost/Schedule Control Systems Criteria (C/SCSC) (35)	INDUSTRY Earned Value Management System (EVMS) (32)
REVISIONS & ACCESS TO DATA: 6	**REVISIONS & DATA MAINTENANCE: 5**
1. Incorporate contractual changes expeditiously, recording the effects of such changes in budgets and schedules. In the directed effort prior to negotiation of a change, base such revisions on the amount estimated and budgeted to the functional organizations.	28. Incorporate authorized changes in a timely manner, recording the effects of such changes in budgets and schedules. In the directed effort prior to negotiation of a change, base such revisions on the amount estimated and budgeted to the program organizations
2. Reconcile original budgets for those elements of the work breakdown structure identified as priced line items in the contract, and for those elements at the lowest level in the program work breakdown structure, with current performance measurement budgets in terms of changes to the authorized work and internal replanning in the detail needed by management for effective control.	29. Reconcile current budgets to prior budgets in terms of changes to the authorized work and internal replanning in the detail needed by management for effective control.
3. Prohibit retroactive changes to records pertaining to work performed that would change previously reported amounts for direct costs, indirect costs, or budgets, except for correction of errors and routine accounting adjustments.	30. Control retroactive changes to records pertaining to work performed that would change previously reported amounts for actual costs, earned value, or budgets. Adjustments should be made only for correction of errors, routine accounting adjustments, effects of customer or management directed changes, or to improve the baseline integrity and accuracy of performance measurement data.
4. Prevent revisions to the contract budget base except for Government-directed changes to contractual effort.	31. Prevent revisions to the program budget except for authorized changes.
5. Document internally the changes to the performance measurement baseline and notify expeditiously the procuring activity through prescribed procedures.	32. Document changes to the performance measurement baseline.
6. Provide the Contracting Officer and the Contracting Officer's authorized representatives with access to the information and supporting documentation necessary to demonstrate compliance with the cost/schedule control systems criteria.	**This Criterion was cancelled.**

References

Chapter 1

Software Technology Support Center. 1999. *Crosstalk, the Journal of Defense Software Engineering* (July).

Chapter 3

Archibald, Russell D., and Richard L. Villoria. 1967. *Network-Based Management Systems (PERT/CPM)*. New York: John Wiley & Sons, Inc.

Driessnack, Lt. Gen. Hans. 1990. How It Started. *PMA Newsletter* (March)

——. 1993. Interview. (July 3).

Moski, Bruno A., Jr. 1951. *Cost Control Fundamentals*. In *Plant Executives' Deskbook*. New York: McGraw-Hill Publishing Co.

Office of the Secretary of Defense and National Aeronautics and Space Administration. 1962. *DOD and NASA Guide PERT COST*. Washington, D.C.

Special Projects Office, Bureau of Ordnance, Department of the Navy. 1958. *Project PERT*. Washington, D.C.

Chapter 4

Beach, Chester Paul, Jr. 1990. A-12 Administrative Inquiry memorandum (November 28). Studies by Gaylord E. Christle, et al. Department of Navy: Office of the Under Secretary of Defense for Acquisitions. (This study cited over 400 programs since 1977. Updates of this same study have increased the sample to over 700 programs without change to the conclusions. Washington, D.C.)

Christensen, Maj. David S., Ph.D., and Captain Scott R. Heise, USAF. 1993. Cost Performance Index Stability. *National Contract Management Association Journal*.

Chapter 5

Archibald, Russell D. 1976. *Managing High-Technology Programs and Projects.* New York: John Wiley & Sons.

Olde Curmeudgeon. 1994. PM 101: The WBS. *PM Network* (December).

PMI Standards Committee. 1996. *A Guide to the Project Management Body of Knowledge (PMBOK® Guide).* Upper Darby, PA: Project Management Institute.

United States Department of Defense. 1967. *Performance Measurement for Selected* Acquisitions. Instruction DOD 7000.2 (December 22). Enclosure 1. Washington, D.C.

United States Department of Energy. 1992. *Project Control System Guidelines Implementation Reference Manual.* (November). Washington, D.C.

Chapter 6

Archibald, Russell D. 1976. *Managing High-Technology Programs and Projects.* New York: John Wiley & Sons.

Canadian General Standards Board. 1993. Policy 187-GP-1 (August) Cost/Schedule Performance Management Standard.

Fitzgerald, A. E. 1967. The Air Force Cost/Schedule Planning and Control System Specification: Experience and Outlook. From a speech given to the Armed Forces Management Association (August 29).

National Security Industrial Association. 1996. Industry Guidelines for Earned Value Management Systems (EVMS) (December).

United States Department of Defense. 1996. Earned Value Management Implementation Guide (December). Washington, D.C.

United States Department of Energy. 1992. Notice DOE 4700.5 (August 21) Project Control System Guidelines. Washington, D.C.

Chapter 7

Archibald, Russell D. *Managing High-Technology Programs and Projects.* 1992. New York: John Wiley & Sons. Quoting from Parkinson, C.N. *Parkinson's Law,* 1957. Boston: Houghton Miffin.

Loh, John M., Lt. Gen. U.S.A.F. Aeronautical Systems Division. 1990. Organizational Alignment to Implement Integrated Product Development, a policy memorandum (March 26). Dayton, Ohio.

National Security Industrial Association. 1996. Industry Guidelines for Earned Value Management Systems (EVMS) (December).

Peters, Tom. 1992. *Liberation Management.* New York: Alfred A. Knopf.

Slade, Bernard N. 1993. *Compressing the Product Development Cycle.* New York: AMACOM Division of the American Management Association.

United States Department of Defense. 1989. C/SCSC Supplemental Guidance Item #4 (July 1989). Washington, D.C.

Chapter 8

National Security Industrial Association. 1996. Industry Guidelines for Earned Value Management Systems (EVMS) (December).

Chapter 9

Arthur D. Little Company. 1986. Survey Relating to the Implementation of Cost/Schedule Control Systems Criteria Within the Department of Defense and Industry. Office of Secretary of Defense (Washington, D.C.)

Chapter 10

Christensen, Maj. David S., Ph.D, USAF. 1994. Using Performance Indices to Evaluate the Estimate at Completion. *Journal of Cost Analysis* (Spring).

Lewis, James P. 1995. *Project Planning, Scheduling & Control.* Chicago: Irwin Professional Publishing.

United States Department of Defense. 1991. Instruction 5000.2, Part 11, Section B, Attachment 1 (February 23). Washington, D.C.

Chapter 12

Office of Management and Budget. Planning, Budgeting, and Acquisition of Fixed Assets. 1997. Capital Programming Guide, OMB Circular No. A-11 (July).

——. 1997. Principles of Budgeting for Capital Asset Acquisitions.

Appendix I

National Defense Industrial Association (NDIA). Industry Guidelines for Earned Value Management Systems (EVMS) (December 1996).

Appendix II

DOD C/SCSC: United States Department of Defense "Instruction DOD 7000.2" 1967.

Industry EVMS: National Defense Industrial Association (NDIA) 1996.

Glossary of Earned Value Project Management Terms

A ———

ACWP — See **Actual Cost of Work Performed (ACWP)**.

AMR — See **Advanced Material Release (AMR)**.

ANSI/EIA — See **American National Standards Institute/Electronic Industries Association Standard 748 (ANSI/EIA)**.

AUW — See **Authorized Unpriced Work (AUW)**.

Activity — Effort that occurs over a time period and generally consumes resources; sometimes also called a "task."

Actual Cost — A cost sustained in fact, on the basis of costs incurred, as distinguished from forecasted or estimated costs.

Actual Cost Of Work Performed (ACWP) — The costs actually incurred in accomplishing the work performed.

Actual Direct Costs — Those costs specifically identified with a contract or project, based upon the contractor's cost identification and accumulation system. See also **Direct Costs**.

Advanced Material Release (AMR) — A document used by organizations to initiate the purchase of long lead-time or time-critical materials prior to the final release of a design.

American National Standards Institute/Electronic Industries Association Standard 748 (ANSI/EIA) — The industry rewrite of the original thirty-five Cost/Schedule Control Systems Criteria (C/SCSC). The ANSI/EIA Standard was issued July 1998.

Applied Direct Costs — The actual direct costs recognized in the time period associated with the consumption of labor, material, and other direct resources without regard to their date of commitment or the date of payment.

Apportioned Effort — Effort directly related to some other measured effort.

Authorized Unpriced Work (AUW) — Any scope change for which authorization to proceed has been given, but the estimated costs are not yet settled.

Authorized Work — That effort that has been definitized, plus that work for which authorization has been given, but definitized contract costs have not been agreed upon.

B

BAC — See **Budget at Completion (BAC)**.

BCWP — See **Budgeted Cost for Work Performed (BCWP)**.

BCWS — See **Budgeted Cost for Work Schedules (BCWS)**.

BR — See **Baseline Review (BR)**.

Baseline — See **Performance Measurement Baseline (PMB)** and **Contract Budget Base (CBB)**.

Baseline Review (BR) — A customer review conducted to determine, with a limited sampling, that a contractor is continuing to use the previously accepted performance system and is properly implementing a baseline on the contract or option under review.

Bill of Material — A complete listing of all parts and raw materials that go into an article, showing the quantity of each item required to make the unit.

Booking Rates — Rates used to record estimated actual indirect costs to a project. The overhead booking rates are applied to direct labor, materials, and other direct costs.

Bottoms-Up Cost Estimate — See **Engineering Cost Estimate**.

Budget — A fiscal plan of operations for a given period.

Budget at Completion (BAC) — The sum of all budgets allocated to a project. It is synonymous with the term "Performance Measurement Baseline" (PMB).

Budgeted Cost for Work Performed (BCWP) — The sum of the budgets for completed work and the completed portions of open work. BCWP has been replaced by the term "earned value."

Budgeted Cost for Work Scheduled (BCWS) – The sum of the budgets for all planned work scheduled to be accomplished within a given time period. BCWS has been replaced by the term "planned value."

Budgeting – Time-phased financial requirements.

Burden – Overhead expenses distributed over appropriate direct labor and/or material base. See also **Indirect Costs**.

C ———

C/SCSC – See **Cost/Schedule Control Systems Criteria (C/SCSC)**.

C/SPCS – See **Cost/Schedule Planning and Control Specification (C/SPCS)**.

C/SSR – See **Cost/Schedule Status Report (C/SSR)**.

CA – See **Cost Account (CA)**.

CAM – See **Control Account Manager (CAM)**.

CAP – See **Control Account Plan (CAP)**.

CBB – See **Contract Budget Base (CBB)**.

CCDR – See **Contractor Cost Date Report (CCDR)**.

CFSR – See **Contract Funds Status Report (CFSR)**.

CPI – See **Cost Performance Index (CPI)**.

CPR – See **Cost Performance Report (CPR)**.

CTC – See **Contract Target Cost (CTC)**.

CTP – See **Contract Target Price (CTP)**.

CV – See **Cost Variance (CV)**.

CWBS – See **Contractor Work Breakdown Structure (CWBS)**.

Commitment – A binding financial obligation, typically in the form of a purchase order.

Concurrent Engineering – The development of new products with the use of multifunctional teams who work in unison from the initial concept until completion of the product. This process is sometimes called multifunctional or integrated product development teams.

Contract Budget Base (CBB) – The negotiated contract cost value plus the estimated value of authorized, but unpriced, work.

Contract Funds Status Report (CFSR) – A financial report that provides forecasted contract funding requirements.

Contract Target Cost (CTC) – The negotiated costs for the original definitized contract and all contractual changes that have been definitized, but excluding the estimated cost of any authorized, unpriced changes. The CTC equals the value of the BAC plus management or contingency reserve.

Contract Target Price (CTP) – The negotiated estimated costs plus profit or fee.

Contract Work Breakdown Structure (CWBS) – A customer-prepared breakout or subdivision of a project typically down to level 3 that 1) subdivides the project into all its major hardware, software, and service elements; 2) integrates the customer and contractor effort; 3) provides a framework for the planning, control, and reporting.

Contractor Cost Data Report (CCDR) – A Department of Defense report developed to provide contract cost and related data in a standard format.

Control Account – A management control point where earned value measurement takes place. Synonymous with the term "Cost Account" (CA).

Control Account Manager (CAM) – A member of a functional organization responsible for cost account performance and for the management of resources to accomplish such tasks.

Control Account Plan (CAP) – The management control unit in which earned value performance measurement takes place. Was called cost account plan.

Cost Account (CA) – A point representing the intersection of the Work Breakdown Structure (WBS) and Organizational Breakdown Structure (OBS), at which functional responsibility for work is assigned. Cost accounts are the focal point for the integration of scope, cost, and schedule.

Cost Control – Any system of keeping costs within the bounds of budgets or standards, based upon work actually performed.

Cost Element – A unit of costs, typically in the form of direct labor, direct materials, other direct costs, and indirect or burdened costs.

Cost Estimate – The expected costs to perform a task or to acquire an item. Cost estimates may be a single value or a range of values.

Cost Incurred – Costs identified through the use of the accrued method of accounting, or costs actually paid. Costs include direct labor, direct materials, and all allowable indirect costs.

Cost of Money – A form of indirect cost incurred by investing capital in facilities employed on government contracts.

Cost Overrun – The amount by which a contractor exceeds or expects to exceed the estimated costs and/or the final limitation (the ceiling) of a contract.

Cost Performance Index (CPI) — The cost-efficiency factor representing the relationship between the actual costs expended and the value of the physical work performed.

Cost Performance Report (CPR) — A monthly cost report generated by the performing contractor to reflect cost and schedule status information for management.

Cost-Reimbursable-Type Contracts — A category of contracts based on payments to a contractor for allowable estimated costs, normally requiring only a "best-efforts" performance standard from the contractor. Risks for all cost growth over the estimated value rests with the project owner.

Cost/Schedule Control Systems Criteria (C/SCSC) — Thirty-five defined standards that have been applied against private contractor management-control systems since 1967 in order to ensure the government that cost-reimbursable- and incentive-type contracts are managed properly. The thirty-five C/SCSC were superseded in December 1996 by the thirty-two earned value management system criteria.

Cost/Schedule Planning and Control Specification (C/SPCS) — The United States Air Force initiative in the mid-1960s that later resulted in the C/SCSC.

Cost/Schedule Status Report (C/SSR) — The low-end cost and schedule report generally imposed on smaller value contracts, not warranting full C/SCSC.

Cost to Complete Forecast — A forecast by time periods for the completion of contractual tasks. Synonymous with Estimate to Completion (ETC).

Cost Variance (CV) — The numerical difference between the earned value (BCWP) less the actual costs (ACWP).

Critical Path — A series of tasks in a network schedule, representing the longest duration for a project. Any slippage of tasks along the critical path increases the duration of a project.

Critical Subcontractor — A contractor or supplier performing a decisive portion of a project that generally requires close oversight, control, and reporting. Critical subcontractors are designated as a result of customer negotiation or by management direction.

D ———

DR — See **Demonstration Review (DR)**.

Demonstration Review (DR) — The initial formal review of a contractor's management control system to determine whether or not it satisfies the requirements of the C/SCSC.

Direct Costs — Those costs (labor, material, and other direct costs, i.e., travel) that can be consistently related to work performed on a particular project. Direct costs are best contrasted with indirect costs that cannot be identified to a specific project.

Discrete Effort — Tasks that have a specific measurable end product or end result. Discrete tasks are ideal for earned value measurement.

Discrete Milestone — A milestone that has a definite, scheduled occurrence in time, signaling the start and finish of an activity. Synonymous with the term "objective indicator."

E ─────

EAC — See **Estimate at Completion (EAC)**.

ESAR — See **Extended Subsequent Applications Review (ESAR)**.

ETC — See **Estimate to Completion (ETC)**.

Earned Hours — The time in standard hours credited to work as a result of the completion of a given task or a group of tasks.

Earned Value — What you physically got for what you actually spent; the value of the work accomplished; the measured performance; the BCWP.

Engineering Cost Estimate — A detailed cost estimate of the work and related burdens, usually made by the industrial engineering or price/cost estimating groups.

Estimate at Completion (EAC) — A value expressed in either dollars or hours to represent the projected final costs of work when completed. The EAC equals the actual costs incurred, plus the estimated costs for completing the remaining work.

Estimate to Completion (ETC) — Expressed in either dollars or hours; developed to represent the value of the work required to complete a task.

Event — Something that happens at a point or moment in time. A significant event is often called a "milestone."

Expenditure — A charge against available funds, evidenced by a voucher, claim, or other documents. Expenditures represent the actual payment of funds.

Extended Subsequent Applications Review (ESAR) — A formal review performed in lieu of a full C/SCSC demonstration review, when contractor conditions have changed; when: 1) programs change from *one phase to another* (e.g., R&D into production); 2) contractors move programs from *one facility to another*; and 3) contractors make significant *changes to their C/SCSC systems description.*

F ———

Fixed-Price Contracts — A generic category of contracts based on the establishment of firm legal commitments to complete the required work. A performing contractor is legally obligated to finish the job, no matter how much it costs to complete. Risks of all cost growth rest on the performing contractor.

Formal Reprogramming — See **Reprogramming**.

Front Loading — An attempt by a performing contractor to provide adequate budgets for the near-term work, but at the expense of the far-term effort, which will be underfunded. It is an attempt to delay the acknowledgment of a potential cost overrun in the hope that the contractor may "get well" through changes in the contract Statement of Work (SOW). Front loading is often the result of inadequate or unrealistic negotiated contract target costs.

Funding Profile — An estimate of funding requirements.

G ———

G&A — See **General and Administrative (G&A)**.

Gantt Chart — The most common scheduling display, graphically portraying tasks over time, frequently called a "bar chart."

General and Administrative (G&A) — A form of indirect expenses incurred for the administration of a company, including senior executive expenses. Such expenses are spread over the total direct and burden costs for the company.

I ———

IBR — See **Integrated Baseline Review (IBR)**.

IPDT — See **Integrated Product Development Team (IPDT)**.

Implementation Review or Visit — An initial visit by members of the customer C/SCSC review team to a contractor's plant to review the contractor's plans for implementing C/SCSC on a new contract. Such visits should take place within thirty days after contract award.

Independent Cost Analysis — An analysis of program cost estimates conducted by an impartial body disassociated from the management of the program.

Independent Cost Estimate — An estimate of program cost developed outside normal channels, which generally includes representation from cost analysis, procurement, production management, engineering, and project management.

Indirect Costs — Resources expended that are not directly identified to any specific contract, project, product, or service.

Indirect Cost Pools — A grouping of indirect costs identified with two or more cost objectives, but not specifically identified with any final cost objective.

Integrated Baseline Review (IBR) — The newest form of the Department of Defense C/SCSC verification review process, in which the technical staff lead the effort to verify that the entire project baseline is in place, together with a realistic budget to accomplish all planned work.

Integrated Product Development Team (IPDT) — The development of new products with use of multifunctional teams, who work in unison from the conceptual idea until completion of the product. IPDT is sometimes called "concurrent engineering" and is best contrasted with the traditional form of sequential functional development.

Internal Replanning — Replanning actions performed by the contractor for any remaining effort within project scope.

L ———

LOE — See **Level of Effort (LOE)**.

LRE — Latest Revised Estimate; see **Estimate at Completion (EAC)**.

Labor Rate Variances — Difference between planned labor rates and actual labor rates.

Latest Revised Estimate (LRE) — See **Estimate at Completion (EAC)**.

Level of Effort (LOE) — Work that does not result in a final product—e.g., liaison, coordination, follow-up, or other support activities—and that cannot be effectively associated with a definable end-product process result. It is measured only in terms of resources actually consumed within a given time period.

M ———

MPS — See **Master Project Schedule (MPS)**.

MR — See **Management Reserves (MR)**.

Make or Buy — The classification of components on a contract as to whether they will be produced by the contractor (Make) or obtained from an outside source (Buy).

Management Reserves (MR) — A portion of the CBB that is held for management-control purposes by the contractor to cover the expense of unanticipated program requirements. It is not a part of the Performance Measurement Baseline (PMB).

Management Reserve Budget — See **Management Reserves (MR)**.

Master Project Schedule (MPS) — The highest summary level schedule for a project, depicting the overall phasing and all major interfaces, contractual milestones, and key elements.

Material — Property that may be incorporated into or attached to an end item to be delivered under a contract, or that may be consumed or expended in the performance of a contract. It includes, but is not limited to, raw and processed material, parts, components, assemblies, fuels and lubricants, and small tools and supplies that may be consumed in normal use in the performance of a contract.

Milestone — An event, usually of particular importance, i.e., a big event.

Multifunctional Project Teams — See either **Concurrent Engineering** or **Integrated Product Development Team (IPDT)**.

N

Negotiated Contract Cost — The estimated cost negotiated in a cost-plus-fixed-fee contract or the negotiated contract target cost in either a fixed price-incentive contract or a cost-plus-incentive-fee contract. See also **Contract Target Cost (CTC)**.

Network — A logic flow diagram consisting of the activities and events that must be accomplished to reach project objectives, which shows their planned sequence, interrelationships, and constraints.

Nonrecurring Costs — Expenditures against specific tasks that are expected to occur only once on a given program. Examples are such items as preliminary design effort, qualification testing, initial tooling and planning, and so on.

O

OBS — See **Organizational Breakdown Structure (OBS)**.

ODC — See **Other Direct Costs (ODC)**.

OTB — See **Over Target Baseline (OTB)**.

Objective Indicator — See **Discrete Milestone**.

Organizational Breakdown Structure (OBS) — A functionally oriented structure indicating organizational relationships, and used as the framework for the assignment of work responsibilities. The organizational structure is progressively detailed downward to the lowest levels of management.

Original Budget — The initial budget established at or near the time that a contract was signed or a project authorized, based on the negotiated contract cost or management's authorization.

Other Direct Costs (ODC) — A group of accounting elements that can be isolated to specific tasks other than labor and material. Included in the ODC are such items as travel, computer time, and services.

Over Target Baseline (OTB) — A baseline that results from formal reprogramming of an overrun, used only with the approval of the customer.

Overhead — Costs incurred in the operation of a business that cannot be directly related to the individual products or services being produced. See also **Indirect Costs**.

Overrun — Costs incurred in excess of the contract target costs on an incentive-type contract, or the estimated costs on a fixed-fee contract. An overrun is that value of costs that are needed to complete a project over that value originally authorized by management.

P ─────

PAR — See **Problem Analysis Report (PAR)**.

PMB — See **Performance Measurement Baseline (PMB)**.

PV — See **Price Variance (PV)**.

PVWA — See **Planned Value for Work Accomplished (PVWA)**.

PVWS — See **Planned Value for Work Scheduled (PVWS)**.

Performance Measurement Baseline (PMB) — The time-phased budget plan against which project performance is measured. It is formed by the budgets assigned to scheduled cost accounts and the applicable indirect budgets. For future effort not planned to the cost account level, the PMB also includes budgets assigned to higher-level CWBS elements. The PMB does not include any management or contingency reserves, which are isolated above the PMB.

Performing Organization — The organizational unit responsible for performance and the management of resources to accomplish a task.

Period of Performance — The time interval of contract performance that includes the effort required to achieve all significant contractual schedule milestones.

Planned Value for Work Accomplished (PVWA) — An early term for BCWP.

Planned Value for Work Scheduled (PVWS) — An early term for BCWS.

Planned Value — The sum of the budgets for all planned (earned value) work scheduled to be accomplished within a given time period. Also known as the BCWS.

Planning Account — Tasks that have been detailed to the greatest extent practicable, but which cannot yet be subdivided into detailed work-package tasks. Planning accounts can exist at any level above the task level.

Planning Package — A logical aggregation of far-term work within a cost account that can be identified and budgeted, but not yet defined into work packages. Planning packages are identified during the initial baseline planning to establish the time phasing of the major activities within a cost account and the quantity of the resources required for their performance. Planning packages are placed into work packages, consistent with the rolling-wave concept, prior to the performance of the work.

Price Variance (PV) — The difference between the budgeted costs for a purchased item and the actual costs.

Problem Analysis Report (PAR) — A report made by the responsible manager to explain a significant cost or schedule variance, its probable impact on the project, and the corrective actions to be taken to resolve the problem(s).

Project Risk Analysis — An analysis of identified project risks with respect to their impact on cost, schedule, and technical performance.

Progress Payments — Payments made to a contractor during the life of a fixed-price-type contract, on the basis of some agreed-to formula—for example, percentage of work completed as used in construction, or simply costs incurred on most government-type contracting.

Project — A one-time-only endeavor to achieve specific objectives with a precise start and completion date and finite resources to accomplish the goals.

Project Team — See either **Concurrent Engineering** or **Integrated Product Development Team (IPDT)**.

Project Manager — An individual who has been assigned responsibility for accomplishing a specific unit of work. The project manager is typically responsible for the planning, implementing, controlling, and reporting of status on a project.

R ———

Readiness Assessment — A meeting or series of meetings by selected members of the customer C/SCSC review team to a contractor's plant to review contractor plans and progress in implementing C/SCSC in preparation for a full demonstration review.

Recurring Costs — Expenditures against specific tasks that would occur on a repetitive basis. Examples are sustaining engineering, production of operational equipment, tool maintenance, and so on.

Replanning — A change in the original plan for accomplishing authorized contractual requirements. There are two types of replanning effort: 1) Internal Replanning — A change in the original plan that remains within the scope of the authorized contract, caused by a need to compensate for cost, schedule, or technical problems that have made the original plan unrealistic; and 2) External Replanning — Customer-directed changes to the contract in the form of a change order that calls for a modification in the original plan.

Reprogramming — A comprehensive replanning of the effort remaining in the contract, resulting in a revised total allocated budget that may exceed the current contract budget base. Reprogramming is normally another term for "overrun."

Responsible Organization — A defined unit within the contractor's organization structure that is assigned responsibility for accomplishing specific tasks, or cost accounts.

Rolling-Wave Concept — The progressive refinement of detailed work planning by continuous subdivision of far-term activities into near-term work-package tasks.

Rubber Baselining — An attempt by a contractor to take far-term budget and move it into the current period, in an attempt to disguise cost problems. Approach will be to move budget, but without a corresponding value of work, to mask cost difficulties. It is an indicator of a likely cost overrun condition.

S ———

SAR — See **Subsequent Application Review (SAR).**

SLVAR — See **Summary Level Variance Analysis Reporting (SLVAR).**

SOW — See **Statement of Work (SOW).**

SPI — See **Schedule Performance Index (SPI).**

SV — See **Schedule Variance (SV).**

Schedule — A graphic display of planned work.

Schedule Performance Index (SPI) — The planned schedule efficiency factor representing the relationship between the value of the initial planned schedule and the value of the physical work performed, earned value.

Schedule Variance (SV) — The numerical difference between earned value (BCWP) less the planned value (BCWS).

Scheduling — The act of preparing and/or implementing schedules.

Should-Cost Estimate — An estimate of contract price that reflects reasonably achievable economy and efficiency. Its purpose is to develop a realistic price objective for negotiation purposes.

Standard — A term applied in work measurement to any established or accepted rule, model, or criterion against which comparisons are made.

Standard Cost — The normal expected cost of an operation, process, or product, including labor, material, and overhead charges, computed on the basis of past performance costs, estimates, or work measurement.

Standard Time — The amount of time allowed for the performance of a specific unit of work.

Statement of Work (SOW) — A description of a product or service to be procured under a contract; a statement of requirements.

Subcontract — A contractual document that legally defines the effort of providing services, data, or other hardware from one firm to another.

Subsequent Application Review (SAR) — A review by customer personnel to determine whether the contractor has properly applied the C/SCSC to a new contract.

Summary Level Variance Analysis Reporting (SLVAR) — The analysis of performance variances from plan, done at a summary level by the amalgamation of related cost accounts with homogeneous effort, and common problems causing such variances.

Surveillance — A term used in C/SCSC to mean the monitoring of continued compliance with an approved/validated management control system.

T ——

TAB — See **Total Allocated Budget (TAB)**.

TCPI — See **To Complete Performance Index (TCPI)**.

Target Cost — See **Contract Target Cost (CTC)** and/or **Contract Budget Base (CBB)**.

Task — Also called an activity, something that takes place over a period of time, which generally consumes resources.

Team — See either **Concurrent Engineering** or **Integrated Product Development Team (IPDT)**.

Thresholds — Monetary, time, or resource values used as parameters, which, if breached, will cause some type of management action to occur.

To Complete Performance Index (TCPI) — The projected performance that must be achieved on all remaining work in order to meet some financial goal set by management.

Total Allocated Budget (TAB) — The sum of all budgets allocated to a contract. TAB consists of the PMB plus all management or contingency reserves. The TAB will reconcile directly to the CBB.

U ———

UB — See **Undistributed Budget (UB)**.

UV — See **Usage Variance (UV)**.

Undistributed Budget (UB) — Budget applicable to contract effort that has not yet been identified to specific CWBS elements at or below the lowest level of reporting.

Unit Cost — Total labor, material, and overhead cost for one unit of production—i.e., one part, one gallon, one pound, and so on.

Unpriced Changes — Authorized but unnegotiated changes to the contract.

Usage — The number of units or dollars of an inventory item consumed over a period of time.

Usage Variance (UV) — The difference between the budgeted quantity of materials and the actual quantity used.

V ———

VAC — See **Variance at Completion (VAC)**.

Validation — A term used in C/SCSC to mean "approval" or compliance with the criteria.

Variable Cost — A cost that changes with the production quantity or the performance of services. It contrasts with fixed cost, which does not change with production quantity or services performed.

Variance — The difference between the expected/budgeted/planned and actual results.

Variance at Completion (VAC) — VAC is the algebraic difference between BAC and EAC.

Variance Threshold — The amount of a variance that will require a formal PAR, as agreed to between the contractor and the customer. Variance parameters will differ, depending on the function, level, and stage of the project.

W ———

WBS — See **Work Breakdown Structure (WBS)**.

WP — See **Work Package (WP)**.

What-if Analysis — The process of evaluating alternative strategies.

Work Breakdown Structure (WBS) — The WBS is a product-oriented, family-tree division of hardware, software, services, and project-unique tasks that organizes, defines, and graphically displays the product to be produced, as well as the work to be accomplished.

Work Breakdown Structure (WBS) Dictionary — A narrative document that describes the effort to accomplish all work contained in each WBS element. The WBS Dictionary will often result in the project or contract SOW.

Work Breakdown Structure (WBS) Element — A discrete portion of a WBS at any level. A WBS element may be an identifiable product, a set of data, a service, or any combination.

Work-Package Budgets — Resources that are formally assigned by the contractor to accomplish a work package, expressed in dollars, hours, standards, or other definitive units.

Work Package (WP) — Detailed short-span tasks or material items, identified by the performing contractor for accomplishing work required to complete a project.

Work Remaining (WR)— Expressed as the Budget At Completion (BAC) less the earned value accomplished.

Work Team Cost Accounts — See either **Concurrent Engineering** or **Integrated Product Development Team (IDPT)**.

Index

Upgrade Your Project Management Knowledge with First-Class Publications from PMI

THE PROJECT SPONSOR GUIDE

This to-the-point and quick reading for today's busy executives and managers is a one-of-a-kind source that describes the unique and challenging support that executives and managers must provide to be effective sponsors of project teams. *The Project Sponsor Guide* is intended for executives and middle managers who will be, or are, sponsors of a project, particularly cross-functional projects. It is also helpful reading for facilitators and project leaders.
ISBN: 1-880410-15-X (paperback)

DON'T PARK YOUR BRAIN OUTSIDE
A PRACTICAL GUIDE TO IMPROVING SHAREHOLDER VALUE WITH SMART MANAGEMENT

Don't Park Your Brain Outside is the thinking person's guide to extraordinary project performance. Francis Hartman has assembled a cohesive and balanced approach to highly effective project management. It is deceptively simple. Called SMART, this new approach is Strategically Managed, Aligned, Regenerative, and Transitional. It is based on research and best practices, tempered by hard-won experience. SMART has saved significant time and money on the hundreds of large and small, simple and complex projects on which it has been tested. Are your projects SMART? Find out by reading this people-oriented project management book with an attitude!
ISBN: 1-880410-48-6 (paperback)

THE ENTER*PRIZE* ORGANIZATION
ORGANIZING SOFTWARE PROJECTS FOR ACCOUNTABILITY AND SUCCESS

Every day project leaders are approached with haunting questions like: *What is the primary reason why projects fail? How technical should managers be? What are the duties of a project management office?* These haunting questions, along with many more, are just a few of the questions and answers Whitten discusses in his latest book, *The Enter*Prize *Organization*. This book is for seasoned employees, as well as for those just entering the workforce. From beginning to end, you will recognize familiar ways to define the key project roles and responsibilities, and discover some new ideas in organizing a software project.
ISBN: 1-880410-79-6 (paperback)

A FRAMEWORK FOR PROJECT MANAGEMENT

This complete project management seminar course provides experienced project managers with an easy-to-use set of educational tools to help them deliver a seminar on basic project management concepts, tools, and techniques. *A Framework for Project Management* was developed and designed for seminar leaders by a team of experts within the PMI® membership, and reviewed extensively during its development and piloting stage by a team of PMPs.
ISBN: 1-880410-82-6 (Facilitator's Manual Set)
ISBN: 1-880410-80-X (Participant's Manual Set)

THE PMI PROJECT MANAGEMENT FACT BOOK

A comprehensive resource of information about PMI® and the profession it serves. Professionals working in project management require information and resources to function in today's global business environment. Knowledge along with data collection and interpretation are often key to determining success in the marketplace. The Project Management Institute (PMI®) anticipates the needs of the profession with *The PMI Project Management Fact Book*.
ISBN: 1-880410-62-1 (paperback)

PROJECT MANAGEMENT SOFTWARE SURVEY

The PMI® *Project Management Software Survey* offers an efficient way to compare and contrast the capabilities of a wide variety of project management tools. More than two hundred software tools are listed with comprehensive information on systems features; how they perform time analysis, resource analysis, cost analysis, performance analysis, and cost reporting; and how they handle multiple projects, project tracking, charting, and much more. The survey is a valuable tool to help narrow the field when selecting the best project management tools.
ISBN: 1-880410-52-4 (paperback)
ISBN: 1-880410-59-1 (CD-ROM)

THE JUGGLER'S GUIDE TO MANAGING MULTIPLE PROJECTS

This comprehensive book introduces and explains task-oriented, independent, and interdependent levels of project portfolios. It says that you must first have a strong foundation in time management and priority setting, then introduces the concept of Portfolio Management to timeline multiple projects, determine their resource requirements, and handle emergencies, putting you in charge for possibly the first time in your life! ISBN: 1-880410-65-6 (paperback)

RECIPES FOR PROJECT SUCCESS

This book is destined to become "the" reference book for beginning project managers, particularly those who like to cook! Practical, logically developed project management concepts are offered in easily understood terms in a light-hearted manner. They are applied to the everyday task of cooking—from simple, single dishes, such as homemade tomato sauce for pasta, made from the bottom up, to increasingly complex dishes or meals for groups that in turn require an understanding of more complex project management terms and techniques. The transition between cooking and project management discussions is smooth, and tidbits of information provided with the recipes are interesting and humorous. ISBN: 1-880410-58-3 (paperback)

TOOLS AND TIPS FOR TODAY'S PROJECT MANAGER

This guidebook is valuable for understanding project management and performing to quality standards. Includes project management concepts and terms—old and new—that are not only defined but also are explained in much greater detail than you would find in a typical glossary. Also included are tips on handling such seemingly simple everyday tasks as how to say "No" and how to avoid telephone tag. It's a reference you'll want to keep close at hand. ISBN: 1-880410-61-3 (paperback)

THE FUTURE OF PROJECT MANAGEMENT

The project management profession is going through tremendous change—both evolutionary and revolutionary. Some of these changes are internally driven, while many are externally driven. Here, for the first time, is a composite view of some major trends occurring throughout the world and the implication of them on the profession of project management and on the Project Management Institute. Read the views of the 1998 PMI Research Program Team, a well-respected futurist firm, and other authors. This book represents the beginning of a journey and, through inputs from readers and others, it will continue as a work in progress. ISBN: 1-880410-71-0 (paperback)

NEW RESOURCES FOR PMP CANDIDATES

The following publications are resources that certification candidates can use to gain information on project management theory, principles, techniques, and procedures.

PMP RESOURCE PACKAGE

Earned Value Project Management
by Quentin W. Fleming and Joel M. Koppelman

Effective Project Management: How to Plan, Manage, and Deliver Projects on Time and Within Budget
by Robert K. Wysocki, et al.

A Guide to the Project Management Body of Knowledge (PMBOK® Guide)
by the PMI Standards Committee

Human Resource Skills for the Project Manager
by Vijay K. Verma

The New Project Management
by J. Davidson Frame

Organizing Projects for Success
by Vijay K. Verma

Principles of Project Management
by John Adams, et al.

Project & Program Risk Management
by R. Max Wideman, Editor

Project Management Casebook
edited by David I. Cleland, et al.

Project Management: A Managerial Approach, Fourth Edition
by Jack R. Meredith and Samuel J. Mantel Jr.

Project Management: A Systems Approach to Planning, Scheduling, and Controlling, Sixth Edition
by Harold Kerzner

A GUIDE TO THE PROJECT MANAGEMENT BODY OF KNOWLEDGE (PMBOK® GUIDE)

The basic management reference for everyone who works on projects. Serves as a tool for learning about the generally accepted knowledge and practices of the profession. As "management by projects" becomes more and more a recommended business practice worldwide, the *PMBOK® Guide* becomes an essential source of information that should be on every manager's bookshelf. Available in hardcover or paperback, the *PMBOK® Guide* is an official standards document of the Project Management Institute. ISBN: 1-880410-12-5 (paperback), ISBN: 1-880410-13-3 (hardcover)

INTERACTIVE PMBOK® GUIDE

This CD-ROM makes it easy for you to access the valuable information in PMI's *PMBOK® Guide*. Features hypertext links for easy reference—simply click on underlined words in the text, and the software will take you to that particular section in the *PMBOK® Guide*. Minimum system requirements: 486 PC; 8MB RAM; 10MB free disk space; CD-ROM drive, mouse, or other pointing device; and Windows 3.1 or greater.

MANAGING PROJECTS STEP-BY-STEP™

Follow the steps, standards, and procedures used and proven by thousands of professional project managers and leading corporations. This interactive multimedia CD-ROM, based on PMI's *PMBOK® Guide,* will enable you to customize, standardize, and distribute your project plan standards, procedures, and methodology across your entire organization. Multimedia illustrations using 3-D animations and audio make this perfect for both self-paced training or for use by a facilitator.

PMBOK® Q&A

Use this handy pocket-sized question-and-answer study guide to learn more about the key themes and concepts presented in PMI's international standard, *PMBOK® Guide*. More than 160 multiple-choice questions with answers (referenced to the *PMBOK® Guide*) help you with the breadth of knowledge needed to understand key project management concepts. ISBN: 1-880410-21-4 (paperback)

PMI PROCEEDINGS LIBRARY CD-ROM

This interactive guide to PMI's annual Seminars & Symposium proceedings offers a powerful new option to the traditional methods of document storage and retrieval, research, training, and technical writing. Contains complete paper presentations from PMI '92–PMI '97 with full-text search capability, convenient onscreen readability, and PC/Mac compatibility.

PMI PUBLICATIONS LIBRARY CD-ROM

Using state-of-the-art technology, PMI offers complete articles and information from its major publications on one CD-ROM, including *PM Network* (1990–97), *Project Management Journal* (1990–97), and *A Guide to the Project Management Body of Knowledge.* Offers full-text search capability and indexing by *PMBOK® Guide* knowledge areas. Electronic indexing schemes and sophisticated search engines help to quickly find and retrieve articles that are relevant to your topic or research area.

ALSO AVAILABLE FROM PMI

Project Management for Managers
Mihály Görög, Nigel J. Smith
ISBN: 1-880410-54-0 (paperback)

Project Leadership: From Theory to Practice
Jeffery K. Pinto, Peg Thoms, Jeffrey Trailer, Todd Palmer, Michele Govekar
ISBN: 1-880410-10-9 (paperback)

Annotated Bibliography of Project and Team Management
David I. Cleland, Gary Rafe, Jeffrey Mosher
ISBN: 1-880410-47-8 (paperback)
ISBN: 1-880410-57-5 (CD-ROM)

How to Turn Computer Problems into Competitive Advantage
Tom Ingram
ISBN: 1-880410-08-7 (paperback)

Achieving the Promise of Information Technology
Ralph B. Sackman
ISBN: 1-880410-03-6 (paperback)

Leadership Skills for Project Managers
Editors' Choice Series
Edited by Jeffrey K. Pinto, Jeffrey W. Trailer
ISBN: 1-880410-49-4 (paperback)

The Virtual Edge
Margery Mayer
ISBN: 1-880410-16-8 (paperback)

The ABCs of DPC
Edited by PMI's Design-Procurement-Construction Specific Interest Group
ISBN: 1-880410-07-9 (paperback)

Project Management Casebook
Edited by David I. Cleland, Karen M. Bursic, Richard Puerzer, A. Yaroslav Vlasak
ISBN: 1-880410-45-1 (paperback)

Project Management Casebook Instructor's Manual
Edited by David I. Cleland, Karen M. Bursic, Richard Puerzer, A. Yaroslav Vlasak
ISBN: 1-880410-18-4 (paperback)

The PMI Book of Project Management Forms
ISBN: 1-880410-31-1 (paperback)
ISBN: 1-880410-50-8 (diskette version)

Principles of Project Management
John Adams et al.
ISBN: 1-880410-30-3 (paperback)

Organizing Projects for Success
Human Aspects of Project Management Series, Volume 1
Vijay K. Verma
ISBN: 1-880410-40-0 (paperback)

Human Resource Skills for the Project Manager
Human Aspects of Project Management Series, Volume 2
Vijay K. Verma
ISBN: 1-880410-41-9 (paperback)

Managing the Project Team
Human Aspects of Project Management Series, Volume 3
Vijay K. Verma
ISBN: 1-880410-42-7 (paperback)

Earned Value Project Management
Quentin W. Fleming, Joel M. Koppelman
ISBN: 1-880410-38-9 (paperback)

Value Management Practice
Michel Thiry
ISBN: 1-880410-14-1 (paperback)

Decision Analysis in Projects
John R. Schuyler
ISBN: 1-880410-39-7 (paperback)

The World's Greatest Project
Russell W. Darnall
ISBN: 1-880410-46-X (paperback)

Power & Politics in Project Management
Jeffrey K. Pinto
ISBN: 1-880410-43-5 (paperback)

Best Practices of Project Management Groups in Large Functional Organizations
Frank Toney, Ray Powers
ISBN: 1-880410-05-2 (paperback)

Project Management in Russia
Vladimir I. Voropajev
ISBN: 1-880410-02-8 (paperback)

A Framework for Project and Program Management Integration
R. Max Wideman
ISBN: 1-880410-01-X (paperback)

Quality Management for Projects & Programs
Lewis R. Ireland
ISBN: 1-880410-11-7 (paperback)

Project & Program Risk Management
Edited by R. Max Wideman
ISBN: 1-880410-06-0 (paperback)

Order online at
www.pmibookstore.org

Book Ordering Information

Phone: 412.741.6206
Fax: 412.741.0609
Email: pmiorders@abdintl.com

Mail: PMI Publications Fulfillment Center
      PO Box 1020
      Sewickley, Pennsylvania 15143-1020 USA